CYCLES of POVERTY and CRIME in AMERICA'S INNER CITIES

CYCLES of POVERTY and CRIME in AMERICA'S INNER CITIES

Lewis D. Solomon

Transaction Publishers
New Brunswick (U.S.A.) and London (U.K.)

Library of Congress Catalog Number: 2011039765
ISBN: 978-1-4128-4738-4
Printed in the United States of America

Library of Congress Cataloging-in-Publication Data

Solomon, Lewis D.
  Cycles of poverty and crime in America's inner cities / Lewis D. Solomon.
      p. cm.
   ISBN 978-1-4128-4738-4
   1. Urban poor—United States. 2. African Americans—Economic conditions. 3. African Americans—Social conditions. 4. Crime—United States. 5. Inner cities—United States. I. Title.
   HV4045.S68 2012
   364.2—dc23
                                                            2011039765

*In memory of my parents who always encouraged me
and taught me to persevere*

Contents

Acknowledgments

This book had its genesis in an action research project of the George Washington University Law School Small Business and Community Economic Development Clinic led by Prof. Susan R. Jones. I participated as a resource in the workforce development action research project designed to educate law students while helping the local community. Prof. Jones encouraged me to expand the conclusion, Chapter 5, of this book. She also provided helpful comments on and suggestions for improving my draft manuscript. Without the research efforts of Leslidiana Jones, Head of Document Services and Research Librarian, Jacob Burns Law Library, The George Washington University Law School, I could not have written this book.

Introduction

Despite the best hopes of the past fifty years, America continues to experience the problem of black urban pathologies. America's inner cities remain concentrations of the uneducated, the unemployed, the underemployed, and the unemployable. Many fail to stay in school, instead becoming high school dropouts. Others fail to be law abiding, choosing a life of drugs, violence, and crime. Most fail to marry, creating vulnerable socioeconomic units, characterized by single-parent households and children who grow up without a father figure. The black urban underclass remains at the margins of mainstream American society. The disadvantaged have become deeply entrenched in America's inner cities. Unfortunately, the cycle continues to repeat itself generation after generation.

Although the American public seems to have written off a part of the population as "unfit" for a civil society, we must wake up to the great waste of human potential. Even in an era of fiscal austerity and scarce public sector resources, a huge slice of America's human capital remains underutilized. The nation pays in many ways when the potential of many black males remains untapped.

When black males cannot find and sustain stable, legal employment, they lack funds to support themselves and their families. They do not pay taxes; this, in turn, deprives localities of funds and weakens local economies. Their inability to join the economic mainstream further exacerbates the breakdown of the two-parent nuclear family. The prevalence of single-parent, female-headed households reinforces the likelihood of another generation of black youth living in inner city poverty and floundering within inadequate education systems. In total, casualties multiply with ever-spiraling rates of unemployment and incarceration.

It is easy to throw up our hands and say that nothing works given the policy failures of the past fifty years.[1] For me, fatalism is not an adequate response to the complex and interrelated web of issues

1

plaguing inner city black males: joblessness; the failure of the public education system; crime, mass incarceration, and drugs; collapse of two-parent married families often marked by parental neglect; and negative cultural messages. Rather than abandoning the black urban underclass to a life of poverty and despair, this book presents nonfederal government-oriented near- and intermediate-term strategies and programs to rebuild lives and revitalize America's inner cities. The only path to these goals need not be through the public sector. Policies and programs that strengthen families, provide early childhood education, and reform K-12 public schools are, however, beyond the scope of this work.

Overview of the Book

This book consists of five chapters. Chapter 1 focuses on the pathologies in America's inner city neighborhoods. It provides a brief overview of four pathologies: unemployment and underemployment, dropping out of high school, mass incarceration, and unwed motherhood and teen pregnancy. Getting at and treating the root causes of these pathologies represents a difficult policy and programmatic undertaking. Despite the federal government's efforts during the past five decades, neighborhoods of concentrated disadvantage still exist, characterized by a cycle of poverty and despair that continues to repeat itself. The impact of mass incarceration of black males, resulting from the War on Drugs, as well as the impact of socioeconomic class and race on childrearing are highlighted.

Chapter 2 focuses on current federally funded rehabilitative efforts for disconnected youth and adults as well as ex-offenders, who are often unemployed and unemployable. Although no definition of the term "disconnected" (or as sometimes used in this work "at risk") individuals exists, basically they are apart from the worlds of school or work. They are not currently attending school and have not been regularly employed for at least six to twelve months. According to one section of the Internal Revenue Code,[2] a disconnected youth hired in 2009 or 2010 for purposes of the federal Work Opportunity Tax Credit (analyzed in Chapter 2) was someone who: (1) attained age sixteen but not age twenty-five; (2) did not regularly attend any secondary, technical, or postsecondary school during the preceding six months; (3) was not regularly employed during the prior six months; and (4) was not readily employable because of a lack of a sufficient number of basic skills, including a high school diploma or a GED (General Educational

Development) certificate. Children of one (or both) incarcerated parent experience another at-risk factor.

Disconnected youth and adults as well as the formerly incarcerated face a number of barriers in obtaining and retaining employment that pays a living wage. In addition to ex-inmates' criminal backgrounds, these barriers include a limited education (either the lack of a high school diploma or a GED or having a high school diploma but being functionally illiterate), few employable skills, substance abuse and mental health problems, and the lack of affordable housing and transportation. As a result, they are often economically dependent on the public sector or turn to criminal activities. They have the potential for an encounter with (or have already encountered) the legal system—the juvenile or adult criminal justice system—and for females, an unwed, teen pregnancy.

As summarized in this chapter, the federal government's efforts are twofold: facilitating workforce development and prisoner reentry. Workforce development represents the utilization of public sector expenditures, on the federal, state, and local levels, as a strategy for job creation.[3] It seeks to meet local employers' labor force requirements and looks to businesses advising service providers what they need by way of employees. Through programs combining education and training, among other services, a workforce development approach also strives to meet job seekers' needs. By helping individuals prepare for jobs, it assists in addressing the problems of unemployment and underemployment. Building the ability of individuals to participate in the labor market and, thus the mainstream economy, workforce development programs help them reach their potential and achieve economic self-sufficiency.

Prisoner reentry represents another broad concept. According to one expert, the term "prisoner reentry," "...includes all activities and programming conducted to prepare ex-convicts to return safely to the community and to live as law-abiding citizens."[4] Those of all political and ideological persuasions want to prevent recidivism, marked by reincarceration, whether resulting from a technical parole violation by parolees, or rearrest and conviction for a new crime, and at the same time encourage prosocial behavior, including employment and the avoidance of substance abuse.

With respect to workforce development for the disadvantaged, the chapter examines two federal approaches: programs funded through the Workforce Investment Act and various tax and financial incentives. Despite the expenditure of billions of dollars over the years, empirical evidence points to the limited (if nearly nonexistent) positive results achieved by an array of programs, in particular the expensive Job Corps, a residential rehabilitative program for disadvantaged youth.

The chapter next surveys reentry programs directed at offenders and ex-prisoners, focusing on the Second Chance Act and the Federal Bureau of Prison's efforts. After evaluating current federal workforce development programs in terms of their duplication and the need for rigorous empirical evaluation, using control groups, wherever possible, in making resource allocation decisions,[5] the chapter concludes with a brief discussion of the impact of public sector fiscal realities. The current and seemingly ongoing fiscal crises of the American public sector will likely fuel a move away from a government-centric approach, thereby opening a void for community-based nonprofit organizations to fill.

Chapter 3 examines how nonprofit organizations can meet the challenges presented by those with criminal convictions and others disconnected from the American mainstream. In an era of public sector austerity, it advocates foundations, corporations, and wealthy individuals fund comprehensive, rehabilitative strategies, ones that nonprofit entities and social entrepreneurs could implement in the near-term, one or two years. Social entrepreneurs, motivated primarily by social benefit, seek to solve seemingly intractable societal problems currently not being adequately addressed. It presents specific examples as well as empirical evaluations of successful programs undertaken by nonprofit mediating institutions, not part of the public sector.[6] These exemplars provide services in a variety of areas including employment, transportation, and entrepreneurial training. Some even operate small businesses offering transitional jobs. With the likelihood of persistently high unemployment and underemployment levels, at least near-term, those with an entrepreneurial bent may find self-employment an attractive path. Unleashed, trained entrepreneurs may flourish, while job seekers may be unable to find employment. Many of these exemplary rehabilitative programs offer not only demand-driven skills training and job placement assistance but also a comprehensive array of social services for substance abusers and the emotionally disturbed, among others, as well as support provided by mentors. Employment-oriented workforce development programs run by nonprofits do not, however, represent an instant panacea. Successful programs rest on

4

accountability, mission, clarity, and financial stability. Additionally, a need exists for collaboration among programs and service providers. Nonprofits (and public sector agencies) will likely accomplish far less of substance by going it alone.

Successful rehabilitative strategies rest, furthermore, on each participant's motivation to change one's attitude and behavior. Given the motivation to alter one's life, organizations can focus on character training. Even the less fortunate must take responsibility for one's life, from birth to death—learning self-control, consideration for others, and personal responsibility, the notion that one's actions have consequences.

Chapter 4 examines intermediate-term—three to five years—preventive strategies and programs to facilitate employment through skills development. It focuses on vocational (now called career and technical) education in urban high schools, both public and charter. It presents evidence-based research pointing to the positive benefits of a vo-tech approach in terms of increased high school graduation rates and subsequent earnings gains. The prevention of social pathologies is far more effective and efficient than paying for attempted cures through more costly rehabilitation efforts.

Adequately funded skills training in high schools and alternative venues likely represents one of the best techniques to dealing with the repugnance of "acting white" and the lure of the "street" where young black males find negative role models, with the most money and the most women, who tell them drugs and crime are "cool" and low-paying jobs are demeaning. It will assist more black males in graduating from high school with marketable skills, thereby discouraging idleness and helping them become and remain law abiding. No longer will they be confined to the margins of the American economy and society for the rest of their lives.

A brief conclusion, Chapter 5, summarizes how the near-term and intermediate-term approaches, developed in Chapters 3 and 4, respectively, can start providing hope to America's inner city, black underclass and enabling more people to fend for themselves. It then offers three strategies focused on the need to rethink: first, the existing barriers to employment, occupational licenses, and driving encountered by ex-offenders; second, childrearing patterns and toxic neighborhoods; and third, the War on Drugs. Hopefully, inner city black males may be able to succeed in life and extract themselves from an existence characterized by poverty and crime.

Notes

1. For more than forty years this topic has been of interest to me. My bibliography includes Robert J. Fox and others, "Can Man Make a Difference?" *Record of the Association of the Bar of the City of New York* 25, no. 6 (June 1970): 392–406; Lewis D. Solomon and Janet Stern Solomon, "Enterprise Zones, Tax Incentives and the Revitalization of Inner Cities: A Study of Supply Side Policymaking," *Detroit College of Law Review* 1981, no. 3 (Fall 1981): 779–836; Lewis D. Solomon, "Microenterprise: Human Reconstruction in America's Inner Cities," *Harvard Journal of Law & Public Policy* 15, no. 1 (Winter 1992): 191–221; Lewis D. Solomon and Mathew D. Vlissides, Jr., "Faith-Based Charities and the Quest to Solve America's Social Ills: A Legal and Policy Analysis," *Cornell Journal of Law and Public Policy* 10, no. 2 (Spring 2002): 265–302; Lewis D. Solomon, *In God We Trust: Faith-Based Organizations and the Quest to Solve America's Social Ills* (Lanham, MD: Lexington, 2003).

2. Internal Revenue Code §51(d)(14)(ii).

3. John Foster-Bey, "Workforce Development," in *Building Health Communities: A Guide to Community Economic Development for Advocates, Lawyers, and Policymakers*, ed. Roger A. Clay, Jr. and Susan R. Jones (Chicago, IL: American Bar Association, 2009), 252–53. For an overview of workforce development policies and programs see Harry J. Holzer, *Workforce Development as an Antipoverty Strategy: What Do We Know? What Should We Know?* (Washington, DC: Urban Institute, October 2008).

4. Joan Petersilia, *When Prisoners Come Home: Parole and Prisoner Reentry* (New York: Oxford University Press, 2003), 3.

5. The nonprofit, nonpartisan Coalition for Evidence-Based Policy seeks to increase government effectiveness through the use of rigorous evidence about what works. Coalition for Evidence-Based Policy, http://www.coalition4evidence.org/wordpress/ (accessed April 29, 2011). See also Ron Haskins and others, "Social Science Rising: A Tale of Evidence Shaping Public Policy," *The Future of Children, Princeton-Brookings,* Policy Brief (Fall 2009) and Jeffrey Pfeffer and Robert Sutton, "Trust the Evidence, Not Your Instincts," *New York Times*, September 4, 2011, Business Section, 8.

6. An overview of workforce intermediaries, both public sector agencies and nonprofit organizations, was provided in *Workforce Intermediaries for the Twenty-First Century*, ed. Robert P. Giloth (Philadelphia, PA: Temple University, 2004).

1

The Abyss in America's Inner Cities

In America's inner city neighborhoods, crime, poverty, unemployment, unwed motherhood, and teen pregnancy rates are sky-high. Poorly educated in dreadful schools, the black male underclass is ever more disconnected from mainstream society. In inner cities, finishing high school is often the exception for black males, legal employment is scarce, and incarceration has become routine.[1] Endemic crime and the drug culture create formidable problems as do children who are raised in single-mother households where limited resources and parenting skills create barriers to success.

This chapter provides a brief survey of the abyss in America's inner cities, focusing on four dimensions: unemployment and underemployment, high school dropouts, mass incarceration, and unwed motherhood and teen pregnancy. Black males, in particular, are not employed, being educated, or trained in a meaningful manner. Together with class- and race-bound childrearing practices, the web of disadvantages has become deeply entrenched in America's urban neighborhoods filled with seemingly permanent, concentrated pathologies. Despite a multitude of efforts by the federal government for nearly five decades, the cycle continues to repeat itself, generation after generation.

Unemployment and Underemployment

The United States faces a stubbornly high unemployment rate hovering between 8 and 9 percent. Along with the unemployment, there are millions more of underemployed individuals, who work part-time but would like to work full-time, and those who have stopped looking for jobs, so-called discouraged workers, who would take jobs if available. In total, perhaps 19.4 percent or some thirty million Americans were seeking a job in March 2011.[2] In particular, long-term unemployment, that is, an inability to find a job after being out of work for six months or more, a devastating personal experience, suppresses the earnings of those impacted, destroys marriages and families, and devastates communities.

The unemployment rate of blacks is substantially higher than the rate for whites. In the second quarter of 2010, for example, the unemployment rate for black males ages twenty and above was twice as high as the unemployment rate for white males of the same age. This category of black males had an unemployment rate of 17.3 percent, while the unemployment rate for similar white males equaled 8.6 percent.[3] Unemployment reached nearly 16 (15.6) percent for African-Americans generally and a mind-boggling 40 percent for black males between ages sixteen and twenty-four, who were not in school.[4]

With limited, near-term prospects for meaningful, stable employment, some African-American men turn to the illegal drug trade. As a result, whole neighborhoods are engulfed and endangered by the violence among drug-dealing gangs for control of drug distribution areas. In addition to drug trafficking, black males out of the labor force survive off of relatives, girl friends, and petty crime. They cannot save for the future, and do not marry the women they get pregnant or support children they father. Their subculture glorifies swagger over work and education.

High School Dropouts

Black males are more likely than white males to drop out of high school and thus not graduate. In 2008, for example, black males were nearly twice as likely to drop out of high school as white males. In the aggregate, 9 percent of black males dropped out of high school compared with 5 percent of white males.[5] In many inner cities across the nation, nearly one-half of all blacks do not finish high school by age nineteen,[6] a stunning statistic, with few attaining their high school diplomas past their normal graduation dates. Even among those who graduate high school, only 42 percent of black males graduated on time, i.e., by their normal graduation dates, in 2006 versus 71 percent of white males.[7] In the nation's largest, high-poverty urban districts perhaps as few as one-third of all students graduate, with the completion rates among certain disadvantaged groups often still lower.[8]

Dropping out of high school has important negative consequences contributing to a multitude of social problems, particularly increased criminal activity resulting in imprisonment and a higher likelihood of unemployment. As young males, especially young black males, drop out of America's educational system, they are more likely to be embedded in criminal networks that restrict their work opportunities, thereby further increasing their criminal involvement. As a result, they are more likely to drop into the nation's criminal justice system. On any given day, according to some estimates, about one in ten young male high school dropouts is incarcerated compared with one in thirty-five young male high school graduates. The situation is much bleaker for blacks with nearly one in four (some 23 percent) young African-American male dropouts incarcerated, whether in jails, prisons, or juvenile detention centers, on an average day.[9] Others paint an even more hopeless picture. According to one expert, among sixteen- to twenty-four-year-old black males not enrolled in school, about one in three is enmeshed in the criminal justice system, either incarcerated, on probation, or on parole; less than one-half have jobs.[10] One study put the 2008 unemployment rate for young African-American high school dropouts, ages sixteen to twenty-four, at 69 percent, compared with 54 percent for non-Hispanic white dropouts and 32 percent for all high school graduates of the same age.[11]

Among the at-risk youth (ages sixteen to twenty-four) and adults, who are neither employed nor attending school, the global economy has little to offer. Idleness fills their days. For younger ex-offenders, who have dropped out of high school, returning to school is generally unappealing. They would likely be older than their classmates; many public high schools are not anxious for them to return and resume their education. These disconnected males are likely to engage in delinquent behavior or illegal activities to earn money. Criminality often flourishes among these disconnected black males, who participate in the sale of illegal drugs.

The illegal drug trade provides not only a livelihood to the poorly educated and hard-to-employ young black males but also an alternative social order, one valuing toughness, and entrepreneurship. The profits generated by drug dealing make it the most lucrative endeavor for many. Drug dealers, the most financially successful people in many inner city areas, have turned the accepted, mainstream social order upside down.

One noted sociologist documented the dominance of the criminal element in America's inner city neighborhoods. Drug dealers, with their displays of money and power, socialize the young in those areas. By the fourth grade, he estimated, "about three-quarters young students have bought into the code of the street or the oppositional culture"[12] where it is better to be respected, if not feared, rather than loved.

Mass Incarceration

Black males, especially high school dropouts, face mass incarceration or are under the watchful eye of the probation or parole system that marginalizes them from mainstream economic and social life in the United States. Amazingly, estimates indicate that some 29 to 37 percent of adult black males are current or ex-felons.[13] With African-American males, including both high school graduates and dropouts, having a one-in-three chance being incarcerated at some point in their lives[14]—a chilling statistic—a major public policy problem exists.

At the start of 2008, the American penal system—prisons and jails—held more than 2.3 million adults, with one in one hundred U.S. adults behind bars.[15] (Prisons house those serving sentences of one year or more; jails house those awaiting trial or serving sentences of less than one year.) At that time, out of 1.6 million (1,610,446) prisoners incarcerated in federal and state prisons, some 592,000 (591,000) were black.[16]

The change in criminal justice policy propelled the penal system growth with its adverse impact on black males. Over the decades, the War on Drugs, which President Ronald Reagan announced in October 1982,[17] has resulted in a huge increase in the U.S. prison population, with much of the extraordinary growth in incarceration resulting from the huge rise in the prosecution and imprisonment for drug offenses. From 1980 to 1997, for example, the number of people incarcerated for drug offenses increased by 1,100 percent.[18] By the late 1990s, nearly 60 percent of all federal prisoners were drug offenders.[19]

Although whites and black likely use illegal drugs with the same frequency, blacks are more likely to be involved in the highly lucrative, but dangerous, business of drug marketing and distribution.[20] The drug trade is violent. No peaceful means exists to resolve disputes over turf, customers, and prices. Rather, adversaries resolve such conflicts with guns and violence. Thus, the drug trade serves users while destroying inner city neighborhoods and devastating the African-American community. The police typically target these areas where drug dealing is visible and thus easier to make arrests.

Largely because of the War on Drugs, the incarceration rates for black males are astonishing. One in thirty American men between the ages of twenty and thirty-four is locked up; for black males in that age group, one in nine is imprisoned.[21] Overall, the rate of black incarceration is eight times that of whites,[22] with many black men locked away for drug-related crimes.

Imprisonment serves as a rite of passage for many black male high school dropouts. Historically, among black men without high school diplomas, who were born between 1965 and 1969, nearly 60 percent had been in prison by 1999 before they reached age thirty-five.[23] The incarceration rate for black male high school dropouts is more than fifty times the national average for all offenders, with some 60 to 70 percent of that group of blacks born since the mid-1960s spending part of their lives behind bars.[24] Among black male high school dropouts ages twenty to thirty-five, on any given day, more were in custody—34 percent—than were working at paid employment—30 percent—in the middle of the last decade of the twentieth century.[25] In short, "serving time in prison [for black male dropouts]...has become a routine life event on the pathway through adulthood."[26]

Widespread incarceration results in a number of negative consequences for those with criminal convictions who are unable to find stable jobs to support themselves and their families. Doing time is stigmatizing, often for life. Employers are less likely to hire ex-offenders than comparable job applicants. One study found that employers were much more reluctant to hire applicants with conviction histories than any other group of disadvantaged workers. Only about 20 (21) percent of employers surveyed would definitely or probably hire ex-offenders, compared to 93 percent for former or current welfare recipients, 66 percent for those with spotty employment histories, and 80 percent for individuals unemployed for one year or more.[27] In short, the formerly incarcerated represent the least desirable job applicants in the labor market pool, at least from an employer's viewpoint.

A conviction signals employers that an individual may be unreliable, untrustworthy, and even dangerous. Employers bear the burden of workplace theft and violence. They fear legal liabilities that may be imposed resulting from the negligent hiring of ex-inmates who subsequently commit crimes in the workplace.

The conviction penalty is enormous for black males. A prison record, according to one study, reduced a job applicant's success in getting a second-round interview by about two-thirds (64 percent) for blacks.[28]

Ex-offenders also face barriers to employment imposed by federal and state laws and regulations.[29] The most common types of jobs with legal prohibitions against the employment or occupational licensing of ex-inmates are in child care, education, nursing, and home health care, where vulnerable populations, such as children and the elderly, are involved. Legal barriers also prevent those with criminal records from becoming employed in the financial and insurance fields.

Federal law also mandates that states revoke or suspend a driver's license for at least six months as a result of a nondriving-related felony drug conviction.[30] This law makes it difficult to find and maintain employment as well as obtain drug treatment and other health-related services. Essentially, it precludes employment in occupations requiring driving.

Not unexpectedly, incarceration not only reduces ex-offenders' access to steady jobs but also to positions that generate future earnings growth. It also erodes existing job skills as well as the contacts that provide information about job opportunities that others obtain through referral networks.[31] Most black males enter the criminal justice system hard to employ due to a history of unemployment, low educational attainment levels, few marketable skills, substance abuse, mental and physical health problems, and lower measures of cognitive skills as shown on academic tests.[32] Deficient with respect to human capital, they leave correctional facilities even harder to employ. Youth detained in correctional facilities prior to the age of twenty have higher unemployment rates and receive lower wages one or more decades postincarceration.[33] Even if they find a job, adult imprisonment further limits economic mobility later in life. Doing time reduces the wages of black ex-offenders by 12.4 percent in comparison to blacks who were never incarcerated; it also diminishes the rate of wage growth over one's life, for those able to gain employment, by about 30 to 40 percent annually.[34]

Black males with criminal records experience difficulties with respect to the character and quality of jobs they secure. Positions obtained pay poorly, typically at minimum wage, and provide little chance of earnings growth; employment is insecure, marked by high turnover rates.[35]

With incarceration contributing significantly to black male poverty and the marginalization of poor blacks, it furthers the distance between poor and middle class African-Americans.[36] The disproportionate incarceration rate among African-American males has produced a cycle of hopelessness that has crippled a portion of the black community. Ex-offenders, experiencing joblessness and limited economic mobility, are demoralized, with the accompanying lack of motivation for traditional work and a general attitude of alienation resulting in financial disenfranchisement, placing them outside the social mainstream. Many returnees seek illegal sources of income and a life of continued crime, thereby perpetuating the incarceration cycle.

Releasees return to a relatively small number of inner city, barely surviving neighborhoods that continue to experience significant economic and social disadvantages, marked by high levels of unemployment, poverty, and crime as well as the presence of other ex-offenders. For example, two-thirds of all prisoners released in 1996 returned to urban core counties in U.S. cities. Within these core counties, releasees were concentrated in a few neighborhoods.[37] The high concentration of prisoner returnees further destabilizes many of these communities by disrupting social networks, limiting the ability to maintain effective, informal social controls, particularly over their youth, and generally weakening ties among residents. A "tipping point" often occurs in which communities cannot exert positive influences on residents' behaviors. Disorder and chaos increase along with crime and violence.[38]

The high imprisonment rate for black males impacts on the women and children left behind, making the lives of mothers and their offspring more difficult. African-American men cannot assume their roles not only as providers but also as husbands and fathers.

Mass imprisonment makes it more difficult for black females to find husbands and for black children to grow up in stable two-parent families with sound male role models. Because incarceration undermines economic prospects and social respectability, male ex-offenders are less likely to get married or live with the mothers of the children they father.[39]

Incarceration undermines a black male's marriage prospects. A black male without a prison record has a 54 percent chance of getting married by his late thirties, compared to a 43 percent chance for former inmates.[40] Incarceration also reduces marriage among those with low educational attainments. In one study, 32.4 percent of incarcerated, black male high school dropouts remained unmarried by age thirty-nine; without doing time, estimates indicate that the number would fall to 26.1 percent.[41]

In addition to blighting the prospects of black females seeking husbands, thereby inhibiting the formation of two-parent households in inner cities where the ex-offender population is drawn, incarceration destabilizes family life. Parental imprisonment has become the norm for black children. More than one million black children under age eighteen, or one in eleven (and some 10 percent of black children under age ten) in 2000, had an incarcerated father.[42]

Children of incarcerated parents are more likely to exhibit low self-esteem and depression and engage in disruptive behavior at home and in school. They are five times more likely to serve time themselves than children of nonincarcerated parents.[43] However, the causal connection between these various negative consequences and children whose parents have been incarcerated is unclear. Although the question exists whether these adverse consequences result directly from parental incarceration or the nature of family life in these households, the negative impact abounds.

Single Mothers and Teen Pregnancies

The breakdown of the black family is well documented. More than 70 percent of non-Hispanic, African-American children are born to single mothers, specifically, 73 percent in 2009.[44] Black children ages eighteen and under were three times more likely to live in single-parent households than white children in 2008. Nearly two-thirds of all black children lived in single-parent households, and only about one-third lived with two parents.[45]

Women who give birth outside of marriage generally are more disadvantaged. They have lower incomes, lesser educational levels, and greater dependence on public assistance than married mothers.[46] In particular, financial hardship is often the hallmark of the single-parent family making the cost of child raising more difficult. The best predictor of poverty is single motherhood, even more than race, neighborhood, or family background.

A consensus exists that out-of-wedlock childrearing is harmful. The destructive impact of nonmarital childbearing is well documented.[47] The dysfunctionality of single-parent families, even controlling for income, contributes to a host of social ills: juvenile delinquency and crime; failing or dropping out of school; engaging in early and promiscuous sexual activity, thereby repeating the cycle of nonmarital births; developing drug and alcohol problems; and suffering emotional or behavioral problems requiring mental health care. Children born outside of marriage generally face significant disadvantages in educational achievement and personal growth. They have generally lower cognitive and emotional development, greater problems with self-control, and are often diagnosed as hyperactive.

Absent fathers inflict wounds, called "father wounds," on their daughters and sons. Daughters raised by single mothers are twice as likely as those from two-parent families to bear one or more children out-of-wedlock,[48] especially as teenagers. Poorly fathered girls fall victim to poorly fathered boys who prey on the vulnerabilities of females hungering for a father's affection. These young black women search for caring through premarital sex as well as through babies to love them, giving rise to another generation of disadvantaged children.

Special problems exist with respect to unwed teen mothering in comparison with older mothers. These teen mothers are more likely to be high school dropouts, with limited ability to provide for their children financially. Compared to children born to older mothers, children born to unwed teen mothers usually have less stimulating home environments and poorer academic and behavioral outcomes.[49]

In the inner city, a rising generation of young black males are the offspring of the often needy, single-parent underclass. They lack a responsible father (or another stable male) to help nurture them and instill impulse control. Emotionally weak and insecure, poorly fathered males often pursue socially destructive behavior. Unsupervised as adolescents, these young males may act aggressively, with little self-control. Because they can be physically violent and are desirous of immediate gratification, they are more likely to get into trouble with the law. Young men who grow up in homes without fathers are twice as likely as other males to be arrested and incarcerated.[50] They see few examples of men acting as family breadwinners and often grow up unprepared to assume the responsibilities of work and family. They may reach adulthood unsuitable for employment and without prospects, thereby perpetuating the cycle of disorderly schools and drug-infested neighborhoods. They often exist by the "code of the street" and retaliate against anyone who antagonizes or disrespects them, regarding violence as a show of strength. In short, these black males comprise an urban underclass, with few links to mainstream American society.

The Impact of Socioeconomic Class and Race on Childrearing

Class- and race-bound childrearing practices adversely impact the children of poverty-stricken, single mothers. Middle class parents raise their children differently from less affluent parents. These differences, stemming from class and race, translate into distinct disadvantages for children of lower income, black parents in schools, on standardized tests, and at work.

Studies show that the childrearing techniques in middle and upper middle class homes differ from those in working class and impoverished homes and what this means for the future of the children raised in the respective homes. In a pioneering study, children from poor, mainly black families engaged in thousands fewer conversations than children from wealthier, mainly white, families so that by age three, the poorer children had vocabularies one-half the size of their more well-off counterparts. Researchers observed and recorded the verbal interactions in a small sample of forty-two families with newborn children for the first two and a half years of the children's lives.[51] College-educated, professional parents spoke, on average, 2,150 words per hour; children of welfare families heard their parents speak 620 words per hour. By age thirty-six months, these researchers estimated that the children of professional parents had heard their parents speak more than thirty million words. In contrast, children in welfare families heard about ten million words. Also, the kinds of words and statements—discouragements (prohibitions and words of disapproval) versus encouragements (words of praise and approval)—the children heard varied by class. By age three, the average child of professional parents heard many more encouragements and far fewer discouragements—a ratio of six encouragements to one discouragement per hour; welfare children heard far fewer encouragements and substantially more discouragements—a ratio of one encouragement to more than two discouragements per hour. Cumulatively, by age three, the child of a professional heard, on average, about 500,000 encouragements and 80,000 discouragements. Welfare children heard, on average, about 75,000 encouragements and 200,000 discouragements. Leaving aside genetic and other environmental factors, hearing more words and more affirmations is correlated with higher IQs; hearing fewer words and numerous discouragements and prohibitions is associated with lower IQs. By age three, the average IQ score of children from professional families equaled 117; the average IQ of the welfare children was 77. In short, the children of more affluent parents gained advantages from the language their parents used and the attitudes to life their parents conveyed.

Parenting styles impact on children's intellectual development. One large-scale study of parental behavior found that black mothers, as a group, ranked lower on five of seven measures of parenting, from nurturance to the availability of books at home, than white mothers, again as a group.[52] Perhaps the most striking difference again centered on children's exposure to language, what many regard as a critical element of success in school.

Researchers have also examined these class differences in childrearing from a cultural perspective. One study of how parents play key roles in their children's development followed eighty-eight families from a variety of backgrounds, subsequently whittled down to a small sample of twelve, divided into three classes: middle, working, and poor.[53] According to the study, middle class parents typically follow a "concerted cultivation" strategy. Home life involves a lot of talk. These parents generally engage their children in conversations as equals, threat them as young adults and encourage them to ask questions, challenge assumptions, and negotiate rules. In addition to reasoning with their children, these parents tend not to give orders; rather they present choices. They talk to their children in ways to engage, not control, them. These parents generally are deeply involved in their children's lives. They oversee school work and make concerted efforts to provide a variety of learning experiences. Numerous planned and scheduled activities enhance their children's development. These structured, adult-supervised activities teach these children how to function in institutional settings. Children learn how to navigate the world of organized institutions. They gain the intellectual and organization skills requisite to thriving in a global, knowledge-based economy.

In contrast, working class and poor families typically follow an "accomplishment of natural growth" strategy, a laissez-faire approach to childrearing. These parents allow their children much more freedom to fill their afternoon and weekends, characterized by socializing with family and friends, but much less freedom to talk back, question authority, or negotiate over rules. Children are taught to defer adults. As previously seen by other researchers, there is much less talk in these homes. Parents are more likely to issue orders, not offer explanations. They fail to prepare their children for a world in which verbal skills and an ability to thrive in organizations are paramount. As a result, these children are not as well prepared for adulthood and the world of organizations.

Less affluent parents generally do not view their children as improvement projects as middle class parents do. This approach leaves their children at a nearly insurmountable disadvantage in contrast to middle class offspring.

Middle class parents pass on other advantages to their children. They familiarize them with the habits and behavioral styles valued by the educational system and employers. In short, the qualities middle class children develop are generally more highly valued over the ones developed by children of working class and low-income parents. As a result, these children may do worse over their lifetimes, in part, because their parents are more committed to a "natural growth" rather than "concerted cultivation" as their model for childrearing.

A recent study highlighted the impact of children's home environments. Researchers looked at 750 pairs of American twins who were given a test of mental ability at the age of ten months and another at the age of two.[54] At two years old, for children in the poorer households, researchers estimated that the home environment accounted for about 80 percent of the variance in individual mental ability. The socioeconomic status of these children's parents and the accompanying home environment negatively impacted their mental ability, holding back their genetic ability.

In sum, class- and race-bound childrearing practices adversely impact the children of less affluent mothers. Simply put, regardless of their innate, genetic ability, generally speaking, children from higher income families can outcompete children from less wealthy families. Children from poorer families are placed at a competitive disadvantage in America's achievement-oriented society and its knowledge-based economy.

Urban Neighborhoods of Concentrated Disadvantage

As a result of the four seemingly permanent pathologies, unemployment and underemployment, high school dropouts, mass incarceration, unwed motherhood and teen pregnancies, as well as class- and race-bound childrearing patterns, America's inner cities have become more homogenous and to an even greater extent, "concentrations of the poor, the poorly educated, the unemployed and the unemployable."[55] There are fewer and fewer positive adult role models for black children; a relatively small percentage of these children live with their fathers; fewer and fewer adult black males have regular jobs. Youth grow up with little hope for the future. The resulting alienation fuels violence and crime. Inner city neighborhoods become ever more vulnerable to family disarray and community demoralization.

Black children often grow up throughout their childhoods in toxic urban neighborhoods, marked by concentrated poverty and disadvantage. One study found that a majority (62 percent) of black children born between 1955 and 1970, and 66 percent of those born between 1985 and 2000 lived in high poverty neighborhoods, i.e., neighborhoods with at least a 20 percent poverty rate throughout childhood. Furthermore, 84 percent of black children born between 1955 and 1970 came from high disadvantaged neighborhoods, not only in terms of poverty, but also in terms of unemployment, welfare receipt, families headed by a single mother, and racial segregation. For those born between 1985 and 2000, however, the percentage of black children living in high disadvantaged neighborhoods dropped somewhat to 78 percent.[56]

Successive generations of black children being raised in these toxic areas experience limited upward mobility. As members of the under-class, they are stuck in neighborhoods of concentrated deprivation for generation after generation. Low parental income limits their families' relocation to "better" neighborhoods.

In addition to a child's home environment, his or her neighborhood environment serves as an important developmental context, par-ticularly for one's verbal cognitive ability. The verbal skills formed by growing up in inner city neighborhoods of concentrated disadvantage, through repeated exposure to negative cultural factors, stunt one's subsequent growth in the larger society. These toxic neighborhoods alter the development of one's verbal ability producing lingering effects, one study concluded. Researchers followed a representative sample of 750 inner city black children, ages six to twelve, wherever they moved in the United States for up to seven years. The results indicated that living in a severely disadvantaged neighborhood reduced the later verbal ability of these black children as if they have missed one year or more of schooling.[57]

Yet, many poor, inner city neighborhoods are culturally heteroge-neous. They contain a mixture of attitudes and behaviors. A single, cohesive culture shared by nearly all of the residents of these high disadvantage neighborhoods generally does not exist. One study documented the divisions between "decent" and "street" families in a Philadelphia ghetto.[58] In contrast to the "street" families, the "decent" families defined themselves on the basis of their employ-ment in the formal labor market (as opposed to the underground, often illegal economy), their children's discipline and self-control, and the avoidance of deviant behavior, such as violence, crime, and drug use.

A Hidden Abyss

To a large degree, we have put the problems of the black underclass, the "Abandoned" in one journalist's words,[59] out of sight and out of mind, thereby avoiding dealing with these problems and nearly eliminating support for constructive policies, programs, and strategies. Physical realities keep the black underclass from generally disturbing members of the middle and upper classes, who live in a protected bubble. Segregated ghettos exist throughout most of America. Successful people, black and white, settle in pleasant places, in cities and the suburbs, and strive to do the best things for their children. They often live in gated communities with private security forces and guardhouses at restricted entrances. In recent decades, middle class blacks, not liking crime and the lack of decent public schools for their children, have moved to previously all-white urban areas and to the suburbs.

In contrast to inner city neighborhoods, middle and upper class children living in the suburbs, by and large, do not go to school with underclass children. Raised by financially struggling single mothers, these children are often disruptive at school, sometimes aggressive and violent, and sexually precocious. Families living in large cities generally send their children to "safe" private schools, where discipline and good manners prevail.

Urban crime typically does not affect the middle and upper classes. Enclaves exist so that criminals face a harder time getting at the more affluent. Rather, criminals prey on their neighbors. These areas with high crime rates, rows of abandoned stores, and street-corner drug markets generally lack legitimate economic opportunities. With limited connections to stable employment opportunities, many residents serve as negative role models for the next generation of children. Black males, for whom drugs and crime serve as a way of life, increasingly gain moral authority in these communities.

The more affluent seldom visit the decrepit, often deteriorating, inner city neighborhoods, unless they take a wrong turn off an interstate highway. Both whites and more affluent blacks lock their car doors when they drive through inner city areas and go on their way. The black underclass is physical and socially remote, invisible to others.

The next chapter analyzes the rehabilitative policies and programs currently undertaken by the federal government. It examines whether many blacks currently born to single mothers who are raised in poverty and chaotic conditions, with the disorder having a negative impact on academic achievement, character formation, and social skills, can acquire through federally funded second chance efforts the job skills that will give them a reasonably secure and improved future.

Notes

1. See generally, Erik Eckholm, "Plight Deepens for Black Men, Studies Warn," *New York Times*, March 20, 2006, A1.
2. Terry Jones, "Joblessness Far Higher than 8.9% BLS Rate," *Investor Business Daily*, March 23, 2011, A1.
3. Sharon Lewis and others, "A Call for Change: The Social and Educational Factors Contributing to the Outcomes of Black Males in Urban Schools," The Council of the Great Schools, October 2010, 6.
4. Petula Dvorak, "There's no Denying Race is Definitely a Factor in This Race," *Washington Post*, August 31, 2010, B1, B5; David H. Bradley, "CRS Issue Statement on Employment and Training Policy," Congressional Research Service, January 11, 2010, IS40285, 1, placed the December 2009 unemployment rate for black teenagers at 48.4 percent. See also Jason L. Riley, "The NAACP's Unhealthy Tea Party Obsession," *Wall Street Journal*, October 25, 2010, A19.
5. Lewis and others, "Call for Change," 5.
6. Gary Orfield and others, "Losing Our Future: How Minority Youth are Being Left Behind by the Graduation Rate Crisis," Civil Rights Project at Harvard University, 2004, 7, Appendix 4: National and State Graduation Rates, Table E. Black. James J. Heckman and Paul A. LaFontaine, "The American High School Graduation Rate: Trends and Levels," National Bureau of Economic Research, NBER Working Paper 13670, December 2007, 29, concluded that about 65 percent of all blacks leave high school with a diploma and another 5 percent eventually obtain a diploma through various job training and adult education programs. See also Orfield, "Losing Our Future"; Christopher B. Swanson, "Sketching a Portrait of Public High School Graduation: Who Graduates? Who Doesn't?" in *Dropouts in America: Confronting the Graduation Rate Crisis*, ed. Gary Orfield (Cambridge: Harvard Education, 2004), 1–8, 13–40.
    Despite the high school dropout rate for blacks, politicians, including President Barack Obama, give lip service to the notion that everyone should go to college, based on the notion that employment and income have increased for those with college degrees. See, e.g., David Leonhardt, "Even for Cashiers, College Pays Off," *New York Times*, June 26, 2011, Week in Review Section 3. Ever the optimist, President Obama wants all young Americans to complete college so that the United States will have the world's highest proportion of college graduates by 2020. Barack Obama, "Address Before a Joint Session of Congress," February 24, 2009, *Public Papers of the Presidents of the United States*, 2009 Book I-January 20 to June 20, 2009 (Washington, DC: Government Printing Office, 2010), 145–53, at 153.

However, see Daniel De Vise, "U.S. Falls in Global Ranking of Young Adults Who Finish College," *Washington Post*, September 13, 2011, A4.

7. David L. Kirp, "The Widest Achievement Gap," *National Affairs* 5 (Fall 2010): 54–74, at 55.

8. Christopher B. Swanson, "The Real Truth About Low Graduation Rates, an Evidence-Based Commentary," Urban Institute, Education Policy Center, 2004, 1.

9. Andrew Sum and others, "The Consequences of Dropping out of High School," Center for Labor Market Studies, Northeastern University, October 2009, n.p. See also Sam Dillon, "Study Finds that About 10 Percent of Young Male Dropouts are in Jail or Detention," *New York Times*, October 9, 2009, A12; Paul E. Barton and Richard J. Coley, "The Black-White Achievement Gap: When Progress Stopped," Educational Testing Service, Policy Information Center, July 2010, 26, placed the incarceration rate at 26 percent for twenty-six- to thirty-year-old black male high school dropouts born from 1970 to 1974.

10. Kirp, "Widest Achievement Gap," 55–56. See also Peter Edelman and others, *Reconnecting Disadvantaged Young Men* (Washington, DC: Urban Institute, 2006), 24.

11. Sum and others, "Consequences of Dropping Out," n.p. See also Dillon, "Study Finds."

12. Elijah Anderson, *Code of the Street: Decency, Violence, and the Moral Life of the Inner City* (New York: W.W. Norton, 1999), 317.

13. Joan Petersilia, *When Prisoners Come Home: Parole and Prisoner Reentry* (New York: Oxford University, 2003), 10, 107–8.

14. The Sentencing Project, Facts About Prisons and Prisoners, July 2010, n.p. See also Nicholas D. Kristof, "Priority Test: Health Care or Prisons," *New York Times*, August 20, 2009, A23.

15. Pew Center on the States, "One in 100: Behind Bars in America 2008," Public Safety Performance Project, February 2008, 3, 5. At the end of 2007, more than seven million Americans, one in every thirty-one adults, were behind bars, or under community correction supervision (either on probation or parole). Pew Center on the States, "One in 31: The Long Reach of American Corrections," March 2009, 4. See generally, Lauren E. Glaze, "Correctional Populations in the United States," U.S. Department of Justice, Office of Justice Programs, Bureau of Justice Statistics, December 2010, NCJ 231681.

16. William J. Sabol and others, "Prisoners in 2008," U.S. Department of Justice, Bureau of Justice Statistics, June 30, 2010, NCJ228417, 2.

17. Ronald Reagan, "Remarks Announcing Federal Initiatives against Drug Trafficking and Organized Crime," October 14, 1982, in *Public Papers of the Presidents of the United States: Ronald Reagan*, Book II-July 3 to December 31, 1982 (Washington, DC: Government Printing Office, 1983), 1313–17. President Richard Nixon initiated the modern U.S. war on drugs in 1970 with the enactment of the Controlled Substance Act (Public Law 91-513).

18. Glenn C. Lowry, *Race, Incarceration, and American Values* (Cambridge: MIT Press, 2008), 8. See also Alfred Blumstein and Allen J. Beck, "Population Growth in U.S. Prisons, 1980-1996," in *Crime and Justice: Prisons,*

ed. Michael Tonry and Joan Petersilia (Chicago, IL: University of Chicago, 1999), vol. 26, 20–21.

19. Bruce Western, *Punishment and Inequality in America* (New York: Russell Sage, 2006), 58.

20. Ibid., 50.

21. Pew Center, "One in 100," 3, 6.

22. Western, *Punishment*, 16; Becky Pettit and Bruce Western, "Mass Imprisonment and the Life Course: Race and Class Inequality in U.S. Incarceration," *American Sociological Review* 69, no. 2 (April 2004): 151–69, at 152, 160.

23. Western, *Punishment*, 3; Pettit and Western, "Mass Imprisonment," 161, 164; Blumstein and Beck, "Population Growth," 23.

24. Western, *Punishment*, 26, 31.

25. Bruce Western and Becky Pettit, "Incarceration and Racial Inequality in Men's Employment," *Industrial and Labor Relations Review* 54, no. 1 (October 2000): 3–16, at 7; Bruce Western and Christopher Wildeman, "The Black Family and Mass Incarceration," *Annals of the American Academy of Political and Social Science* 621 (January 2009): 221–42, at 225. See also Eckholm, "Plight Deepens," A18.

26. Western and Wildeman, "Black Family," 231, 232.

27. Harry J. Holzer and others, "Employer Demand for Ex-Offenders: Recent Evidence from Los Angeles," unpublished, March 2003, 8, 21, 22. Not unexpectedly the employers surveyed were strongly adverse to hiring ex-offenders incarcerated for violent offenses and less adverse to those convicted of drug and property offenses. Ibid., 14, 21. See also Harry J. Holzer and others, "The Effects of an Applicant's Criminal History on Employer Hiring Decisions and Screening Practices: Evidence from Los Angeles," in *Barriers to Reentry: The Labor Market for Released Prisoners in Post-Industrial America*, ed. Shawn Bushway, Michael A. Stoll, and David F. Weiman (New York: Russell Sage, 2007), 122–23; Harry J. Holzer and others, "Will Employers Hire Former Offenders?: Employer Preferences, Background Checks, and Their Determinants," in *Imprisoning America: The Social Effects of Mass Incarceration*, ed. Mary Pattilo, David Weiman, and Bruce Western (New York: Russell Sage, 2004), 206–15; Harry J. Holzer and others, "Can Employers Play a More Positive Role in Prisoners Reentry?" Working Discussion Paper for the Urban Institute's Reentry Roundtable, March 2002, 3–4, 10, 14 (Table 1 The Willingness of Employers to Hire Workers from Various Stigmatized Groups).

28. Devah Pager, "The Mark of a Criminal Record," *American Journal of Sociology* 108, no. 5 (March 2003): 937–75, at 943, 956–57. In another study, the negative effect of a criminal conviction was substantially larger for blacks than for whites, with 60 percent of the black applicants suffering a criminal record penalty, double the 30 percent penalty for whites with a record. Devah Pager and others, "Sequencing Disadvantage: Barriers to Employment Facing Young Black and White Men with Criminal Records," *Annals of the American Academy of Political and Social Science* 623 (May 2009): 195–213, at 199. See also Devah Pager and Lincoln Quillian, "Walk the Talk? What Employers Say Versus What They Do," *American Sociological Review* 70, no. 3 (June 2005): 355–80; Jennifer Fahey and others, "Employment of Ex-Offenders: Employer Perspectives," Crime

and Justice Institute, October 31, 2006, 2–3; Shelley Albright and Furjen Denq, "Employer Attitudes toward Hiring Ex-Offenders," *Prison Journal* 76, no. 2 (June 1996): 118–37, at 120, 127, 131, 133, 135.

29. For example, federal law restricts the employment of ex-offenders in the financial industry (12 USC §1829), the health care industry (42 USC §1320a-7), and the child care industry (42 USC §13041). In addition to the loss of some aspects of citizenship, such as the right to vote, and bars to certain types of employment, other restrictions imposed on ex-offenders, beyond the scope of this work, include eligibility for public housing, TANF benefits, and food stamps. See generally, Legal Action Center, "After Prison: Roadblocks to Reentry: A Report on State Legal Barriers Facing People with Criminal Records, 2004" and Legal Action Center, "After Prison: Roadblocks to Reentry: A Report on State Legal Barriers Facing People with Criminal Records, 2009 Update." See also Legal Action Center, "Housing Laws Affecting Individuals with Criminal Convictions," n.d. For a state-by-state survey of civil disabilities of convicted felons see Margaret Colgate Love and Susan M. Kuzma, *Civil Disabilities: A State-By-State Survey October 1996* (Washington, DC: U.S. Department of Justice, Office of the Pardon Attorney, 1997).

30. 23 USC §159.

31. Western, *Punishment*, 112–14, 120–22.

32. As to educational levels of black state prison inmates and black male state prison inmates, ages twenty through thirty-nine see Caroline Wolf Harlow, "Education and Correctional Populations," U.S. Department of Justice, Office of Justice Programs, Bureau of Justice Statistics, January 2003, revised April 15, 2003, NCJ 195670, 6 (Table 7 Education, by race/Hispanic origin for State prison inmates, 1997 and White, black, and Hispanic male inmates ages 20 through 39 markedly less educated than their counterparts in the general population).
    Blacks demonstrate lower cognitive skills in terms of student reading and math test scores. Barton and Coley, "Black-White Achievement Gap," 5–7. In an analysis of black–white skill gaps, Derek Neal, "Why Has Black-White Skill Convergence Stopped?," National Bureau of Economic Research, January 2005, 7–16, NBER Working Paper 11090, reported significant differences in racial reading and math achievement. Whether lower test scores result from mainly genetic factors (see, e.g., Richard J. Herrnstein and Charles Murray, *The Bell Curve: Intelligence and Class Structure in American Life* [New York: Free Press, 1994], 276–95, 301–11) or largely environmental factors (see, e.g., Richard E. Nisbett, *Intelligence and How To Get It: Why School and Cultures Count* [New York: W.W. Norton, 2009], 93–118), is beyond the scope of this work. See also Roland G. Fryer, Jr. and Steven D. Levitt, "Understanding the Black-White Test Score Gap in the First Two Years of School," *Review of Economics and Statistics* 86, no. 2 (May 2004): 447–64; Roland G. Fryer, Jr. and Steven D. Levitt, "The Black-White Test Score Gap through Third Grade," *American Law and Economics Review* 8, no. 2 (Summer 2006): 249–81; In *The Black-White Test Score Gap*, ed. Christopher Jencks and Meredith Phillips (Washington, DC: Brookings Institution, 1998), represented the first, serious comprehensive effort to focus on the racial achievement gap as a topic of serious inquiry.

33. Western, *Punishment*, 112; Bruce Western and Katherine Beckett, "How Unregulated is the U.S. Labor Market: The Penal System as a Labor Market Institution," *American Journal of Sociology* 104, no. 4 (January 1999): 1030–60, at 1048–49, 1051.

34. Western, *Punishment*, 119–20, 123–25, 126, 129; Bruce Western, "The Impact of Incarceration on Wage Mobility and Inequality," *American Sociological Review* 67, no. 4 (August 2002): 526–46, at 528, 529, 536–38, 541. See also Bruce Western and others, "The Labor Market Consequences of Incarceration," *Crime & Delinquency* 47, no. 3 (July 2001): 410–27.

35. Western, *Punishment*, 125–26.

36. Ibid., 127–29, 194.

37. James P. Lynch and William J. Sabol, "Prisoner Reentrying Perspective," Urban Institute, Crime Policy Report Volume 3, September 2001, 15 (Figure 7 Estimated percentage of offenders released into core counties, by type of release, 1984, 1996) and 16.

38. Jeremy Travis and others, "From Prison to Home: The Dimensions and Consequences of Prisoner Reentry," Urban Institute, June 2001, 40–42.

39. Leonard M. Lopoo and Bruce Western, "Incarceration and the Formation and Stability of Marital Unions," *Journal of Marriage and Family* 67, no. 3 (August 2005): 721–34; Christopher Uggen and others, "Work and Family Perspectives on Reentry," in *Prisoner Reentry and Crime in America*, ed. Jeremy Travis and Christy Visher (New York: Cambridge University, 2005), 221–23.

40. Western, *Punishment*, 145.

41. Ibid., 149–51.

42. Western and Wildeman, "Black Family," 235. For black children with high school dropout parents, about half of their parents were imprisoned in the early years of the first decade of this century. Ibid., 236.

43. Petersilia, *When Prisoners Come Home*, 8, 43–44. See also John Hagan and Ronit Dinovitzer, "Collateral Consequences of Imprisonment for Children, Communities, and Prisoners," *Crime and Justice* 26 (1999): 121–62, at 144–48; Christopher J. Mumola, "Incarcerated Parents and Their Children," U.S. Department of Justice, Office of Justice Programs, Bureau of Justice Statistics, August 2000, NCJ 182335.

44. Child Trends, "DataBank, Percentage of Births to Unmarried Women," n.d. http:// www.childtrendsdatabank.org (accessed February 22, 2011).

45. Lewis and others, "Call for Change," 3. Other commentators have indicated that about one-half (54 percent) of all African-American children are raised in single-mother households without a father on the premises. Eugene Robinson, *Disintegration: The Splintering of Black America* (New York: Doubleday, 2010), 130.

46. Elizabeth Terry-Humen and others, "Births Outside Marriage: Perceptions vs. Reality," Child Trends Research Brief, April 2001, n.p.; Anne K. Driscol and others, "Non-Marital Childbearing among Adult Women," *Journal of Marriage and Family* 61, no. 1 (February 1999): 178–87, at 182–86.

47. Sara McLanahan and Gary Sandefur, *Growing up with a Single Parent: What Hurts, What Helps* (Cambridge: Harvard University, 1994), 19–63; William S. Aquilino, "The Life Course of Children Born to Unmarried Mothers: Childhood Living Arrangements and Young Adult Outcomes,"

Journal of Marriage and Family 58, no. 2 (May 1996): 293–310; Robert Haveman and others, "Intergenerational Effects of Non-Marital and Early Childbearing," in *Out of Wedlock: Causes and Consequences of Non-Marital Fertility*, ed. Lawrence L. Wu and Barbara Wolfe (New York: Russell Sage, 2001), 287–315.

48. James Q. Wilson, *The Marriage Problem? How Our Culture Has Weakened Families* (New York: HarperCollins, 2002), 7.

49. Jennifer S. Manlove and others, "Outcomes for Children of Teen Mothers from Kindergarten through Adolescence," in *Kids Having Kids: Economic Costs and Social Consequences of Teen Pregnancy*, ed. Saul D. Hoffman and Rebecca A. Maynard, 2nd ed. (Washington, DC: Urban Institute, 2008), 170–80; Judith A. Levine and others, "Academic and Behavioral Outcomes among the Children of Young Mothers," *Journal of Marriage and Family* 63, no. 2 (May 2001): 355–69.

50. Maggie Gallagher, "Fatherless Boys Grow up into Dangerous Men," *Wall Street Journal*, December 1, 1998, A22. See also Cynthia Harper and Sara S. McLanahan, "Father Absence and Youth Incarceration," *Journal of Research on Adolescence* 14, no. 3 (September 2004): 369–97, at 387–88; Amy Conseur, "Maternal and Prenatal Risk Factors for Later Delinquency," *Pediatrics* 99, no. 6 (June 1997): 785–90, at 786.

51. The statistics in this paragraph are from Betty Hart and Todd R. Risley, *Meaningful Differences in the Everyday Experience of Young American Children* (Baltimore, MD: Paul H. Brookes, 1995), 132, 163, 197–200. See also Clayton M. Christensen and others, *Disrupting Class: How Disruptive Innovation Will Change the Way the World Learns* (New York: McGraw Hill, 2008), 149–50.

52. Jean Brooks-Gunn and Lisa B. Markham, "The Contribution of Parenting to Ethnic and Racial Gaps in School Readiness," *The Future of Children* 15, no. 1 (Spring 2005): 139–68, at 149–50.

53. See generally, Annette Lareau, *Unequal Childhoods: Class, Race, and Family Life* (Berkeley, CA: University of California, 2003).

54. Elliot M. Tucker-Drob and others, "Emergence of a Genex Socioeconomic Status Interaction on Infant Mental Ability between 10 Months and 2 Years," *Psychological Science* 22, no. 1 (January 2011): 125–33. See also Jonah Lehrer, "Why Rich Parents Don't Matter," *Wall Street Journal*, January 22–23, 2011, C12.

55. Nathan Glazer, "Notes on the State of Black America," *American Interest* 5, no. 6 (July/August 2010): 110–16, at 112.

56. The statistics in this paragraph are from Patrick Sharkey, "Neighborhoods and the Black-White Mobility Gap," Pew Memorial Trusts, Economic Mobility Project, July 2009, 9–10. See also Patrick Sharkey, "The Intergenerational Transmission of Context," *American Journal of Sociology* 113, no. 4 (January 2008): 931–69; Robert J. Sampson and others, "Assessing 'Neighborhood Effects': Social Processes and New Directions in Research," *Annual Review of Sociology* 28 (2002): 443–78; Alec MacGillis, "Neighborhoods Key to Future Income, Study Finds," *Washington Post*, July 27, 2009, A6.

57. Robert J. Sampson and others, "Durable Effects of Concentrated Disadvantage on Verbal Ability among African-American Children," *Proceedings*

of the National Academy of Sciences 105, no. 3 (January 22, 2008): 845–52.

58. Anderson, *Code of the Street*, 32–53, 311–20.
59. Robinson, *Disintegration*, 107–38.

2

Current Federal Rehabilitative Workforce Development and Prisoner Reentry Policies and Programs: An Overview

Federally funded workforce development programs exist for the hard-to-employ, including the disconnected and the formerly incarcerated. As noted in Chapter 1, those with a criminal past face special problems in seeking and gaining employment. However, the number of ex-offenders continues to grow. In 2009, for example, nearly 730,000 (729,295) individuals were released from federal and state prisons.[1] States cannot afford to devote huge portions of dwindling budgets to fund incarceration. Thus, to save money on correctional programs and reduce overcrowding, in coming years states will likely boost the number of paroled prisoners, thereby returning more ex-inmates to the streets.

Most ex-offenders fail to navigate reentry successfully. In 1994, for example, more than two-thirds (67.5 percent) of those released from prisons in fifteen states were rearrested for new crimes within three years from their release. More than half (51.8 percent) returned to prison as a result of another sentence for a new crime or a technical parole violation.[2] The period immediately following release is critical to long-term success. Nearly 30 percent (29.9 percent) of all the 1994 releasees were rearrested within six months postrelease.[3] The younger the prisoner, the higher the rate of recidivism, with more than 80 percent of those under age eighteen rearrested within three years versus 45.3 percent of those forty-five or older.[4]

Employment, substance abuse treatment, marriage, the support of family, peers, and the community are important to reentry success.[5] In particular, employment reduces recidivism among ex-prisoners.[6]

Finding a job is critical to successful reintegration. Steady work at decent wages brings money to support one's self (and one's family) and pay debts, including child support, thereby lessening the temptation to seek illegal means to earn money. Employment helps connect ex-prisoners with positive social networks and provides a structured, daily routine. The workplace with its supervisory mechanisms and its behavioral requirements provides a type of social control. Being an employee fosters a prosocial identity linked to leaving behind one's past criminal identity.[7]

This chapter analyzes current federal workforce development and prisoner reentry policies and programs. With respect to workforce development for the disadvantaged, including ex-inmates, it examines two federal approaches: four programs funded through the Workforce Investment Act (WIA), namely, adult program, youth activities, Job Corps, and YouthBuild, and three types of tax and financial incentives for employers, namely, the Work Opportunity Tax Credit, the Empowerment Zone Employment Tax Credit (EZEC), and the Federal Bonding Program. Despite expenditure of billions of dollars over the years, the best empirical evidence demonstrates that there are limited, if any, significant, positive results achieved by those programs, in particular, the expensive Job Corps effort.

The chapter next surveys reentry programs directed at offenders and those with criminal convictions, focusing on the Second Chance Act (SCA). The Federal Bureau of Prisons (BOP) reentry programs, particularly its work and job skills efforts, are summarized, together with pioneering research showing that these programs reduced recidivism.

The chapter then evaluates current federal workforce development programs in terms of their duplication and the need for rigorous evaluation. After considering the possibilities raised by a new funding mechanism, social impact bonds, the chapter concludes with a brief discussion of the current public sector fiscal realities and their consequences, as well as recommendations to improve the effectiveness of federal workforce development programs.

Current Federal Workforce Development Programs for the Disadvantaged Including the Formerly Incarcerated

The federal government currently funds a number of employment and job training programs for the disadvantaged, including ex-offenders, notably through the WIA. The federal government also offers tax credits and other financial incentives for employers to hire the disadvantaged. State and local employment and job training programs for the hard-to-employ are, however, beyond the scope of this book.

The federal government has long funded rehabilitative employment and job training programs for disconnected adults and youths. The latest embodiment, the WIA,[8] enacted in 1998, currently constitutes the nation's primary public workforce development system through which individuals, both disconnected adults and youths as well as ex-offenders, may access various labor-market programs and services. It serves as a universal system for adults, youth, and dislocated workers, with different funding streams for each group. The last group is, however, beyond the scope of this book.

Although not unifying all federal initiatives, the WIA consolidated more than sixty previous federal employment and job training programs into a series of formula block grants to the states. In enacting the WIA, Congress sought to encourage collaboration among workforce, industry, and education partners as well as economic development efforts in the states and localities through the creation of Workforce Investment Boards (WIBs).

The WIA mandates the establishment of state and local WIBs.[9] To better meet the labor needs of employers, business representatives sit on these state and local boards and serve as board chairs. State boards assist each governor in developing the state's five-year strategic plan for providing state-specific employment and job training services, among other functions. Local boards perform multiple functions, including the formulation of a local plan for workforce development to enhance employment and job training opportunities in conjunction with the state's plan. Each local WIB strives to work with local social service providers (both governmental and nongovernmental) and the private sector to oversee an effective workforce development strategy to increase occupational skills, work readiness, and access to the labor market, thereby improving the quality of the nation's workforce, reducing welfare dependency, and increasing participants' employment, job retention, and earnings.

Local service delivery areas exist throughout each state, with more than 600 workforce investment areas nationwide. A One-Stop delivery system exists within each local workforce investment area. Each local area must have at least one bricks-and-mortar One-Stop Center, as designated or certified by the local WIB.

The consolidation of major federal employment and job training programs through a single delivery system, the One-Stop system, represents the WIA's hallmark.[10] The One-Stop Centers provide employment and job training service delivery for adults and, generally speaking, disadvantaged youths (including ex-offenders) and serve both job seekers and employers in one location. In short, the One-Stop Centers provide a single, integrated point of contact for individuals and businesses to access WIA-funded services and those of its various partner programs, thereby facilitating the more efficient delivery of assistance.

Adult Program

For adults, eighteen years and older, the One-Stop system, offering a full array of employment-related services under one roof, provides core services and access to intensive services and authorized training services. As administered by the U.S. Department of Labor, each One-Stop Center provides core services, available to all adults and youths, ages nineteen to twenty-one, receiving services under adult funding. The core services offered include initial skills assessment, job search and job placement assistance, and information about the local labor market. These services consist basically of low-cost job search assistance through computerized job banks (more technically, public labor exchanges) where individuals identify relevant job openings posted by firms.

The three levels of services offered to individuals, namely, core, intensive, and training, are provided sequentially. To be eligible for the higher cost, more individualized intensive services, an individual must first receive at least one core service and have been unable to obtain or retain employment. The intensive services include comprehensive and specialized skills assessments, diagnostic testing, development of an individual employment plan, individual (or group) counseling and career planning, and case management services.

To be eligible to receive training services, an individual must have received at least one intensive service and be unable to obtain or retain employment. Training services include occupational skills training, skills upgrading and retraining, and job readiness training. Participants receive training services from authorized providers designated by a local WIB through individual training accounts. The qualified training providers furnish One-Stop Center operators with information about their training programs and outcomes. Seeking to empower job seekers through materials about training programs, the operators make the information available to participants, who use it to choose the qualified training program that best meets their individual needs to attain employment. Once a participant selects a training provider, the One-Stop Center assumes responsibility for paying the provider through his or her individual training account, consisting of a voucher-like instrument, with the states having flexibility to determine how much each voucher is worth.

In seeking to provide a combination of services to improve an individual's employment opportunities, the One-Stop Centers focus on the inexpensive core services and avoid more costly efforts.[11] About 97 percent of the adults served by the One-Stop system receive only core services at a cost of about $50 per person in the form of job search help, labor market information, and job referrals. Only 3 percent receive the more costly intensive services, which at about $5,000 per person, absorb about 75 percent of the One-Stop system's funds.[12] One-Stop intensive and training programs need not serve every person eligible for assistance and often lack funds to do so, reserving monies for low-income individuals if funds are insufficient to serve everyone. As a result, the One-Stop Centers emphasize a "work first" approach, placing adults in employment as quickly and cheaply as possible, with the least degree of intervention needed for job placement, by providing low-cost information.

Youth Activities

Under the WIA youth programs, administered by the U.S. Department of Labor, youths receive assessments and services that provide them with education, skills training, and various supportive services.[13] In addition to generally meeting a low-income requirement, eligible youth must be between fourteen and twenty-one and face one or more of six employment barriers, including a deficiency in basic literacy skills, a school dropout, homeless, pregnant (or parenting), an ex-offender, or someone requiring additional assistance to complete an educational program or to secure and hold employment. The program assists both in-school and out-of-school youth, with a focus on dropout prevention for in-school youth who are less expensive to serve than out-of-school youth.

All youth programs must provide ten activities (so-called program elements) grouped around four major themes: first, improving education's achievement (tutoring, study skills training, and instruction leading to high school completion, including dropout prevention strategies; alternative high school services, as appropriate); second, preparing for and succeeding in employment (summer employment opportunities directly linked to academic and occupational learning, as appropriate; paid and unpaid work experiences, including internships and job shadowing; occupational skill training, as appropriate); third, developing potential citizens and leaders (leadership development opportunities); and fourth, supporting youth (supportive services; adult mentoring for the participation period, and a subsequent period, for a total of not less than twelve months; comprehensive guidance and counseling, which may include drug and alcohol abuse counseling and referral, as appropriate; and follow-up services for not less than twelve months after the completion of participation, as appropriate). Although local WIBs must make all of those elements available, either through approved youth service providers or the One-Stop system, each individual need not participate in all ten elements. In addition to helping disadvantaged youth gain access to the various program elements, the One-Stop system provides all youth with basic core services, whether or not they are eligible for the youth activities under WIA.

Generally speaking, youth activities, in contrast to the adult program, represent a move away from short-term interventions, represented by the core services for adults, toward a longer-term development approach. The youth program focuses on more basic outcomes, such as the attainment of work readiness and occupational skills, with the development of a unique strategy for each participant.

Evaluating the Adult Program and the Youth Activities

Over the years, the federal government has spent billions of dollars on WIA programs for adults and disadvantaged youth, including ex-offenders. Funding for the adult program and the youth activities runs to somewhat under one billion dollars each, about $770 million ($771,040,000) in fiscal year 2011, down from some $860 million ($861,540,000) in fiscal year 2010, and about $827 million ($827,569,000) in fiscal year 2011, down from some $924 million ($924,069,000) in fiscal year 2010, respectively. In addition, the Employment Service program provides core services at One-Stop Centers at a cost of nearly one and a quarter billion dollars ($1,224 billion) annually.

Despite the existence of performance standards for the adult program and the youth activities, these programs lack rigorous evaluation.

Emphasizing various outcomes, Congress specified core performance indicators for the WIA's adult program and for older youths, ages nineteen to twenty-one.[14] Accountability measures include entry by participants into unsubsidized employment, retention in unsubsidized employment six months after entry into the workforce, earnings received in unsubsidized employment six months after entry into employment, and the attainment of recognized educational/occupational credentials. The adult indicators apply to older youth served under the adult funding stream with the educational/occupational rate applicable to entry into postsecondary education, advanced training, or unsubsidized employment. There are also core performance indicators for youths (ages fourteen to eighteen), including high school diploma or equivalent attainment rate, skills attainment rate, and placement and retention rate in postsecondary education or advanced training, or placement and retention rate in military service, employment, or qualified apprenticeships.[15] The WIA also sets forth customer service indicators, namely, employers' and participants' evaluations of the services received.[16] However, Congress described these performance measures in general terms, allowing states and localities to define programmatic success on their own terms, subject to the agreement by the Department of Labor for states and each state's governor for the localities.[17]

Because program impact evaluations have not been performed and collected, performance outcome data are reliable; little is known about the effectiveness of the WIA adult program and youth activities. Impact evaluations provide useful information on programmatic effectiveness by distinguishing between outcomes resulting from a program itself and those resulting from extrinsic factors. In 2005, the U.S. Office of Management and Budget, using its Program Assessment Rating Tool, assigned the WIA adult program an overall rating of "adequate," one step above "ineffective." Although the report indicated that the adult program met its central goals of helping participants find jobs and keep them, the adult program received a zero score for its independent evaluation efforts.[18] As to youth activities, a 2004 report by the U.S. General Accounting Office concluded, "Robust research and reliable performance data are needed to obtain a complete picture of the WIA youth program's effectiveness and outcomes and to make quality decision about managing the program. However, none currently [as of February 2004] exist."[19] Specifically, the performance data submitted by the states to the U.S. Department of Labor were not sufficiently reliable to determine the outcomes for the WIA youth program.

The Department of Labor has failed to timely implement a congressionally mandated experimental evaluation using a random assignment design. The WIA required at least one large-scale, multisite evaluation of Department of Labor workforce development programs by September 2005.[20] In November 2007, the Department of Labor submitted a request for proposals for the evaluation to be completed in 2015. This void left the U.S. Government Accountability Office (GAO) to conclude:

> Despite the progress that has been made in improving the system's performance data, little is known about what the workforce system is achieving. [The Department of] Labor has not made such research a priority and, consequently, is not well positioned to help workers or policymakers understand which employment and training approaches work best. Knowing what works for whom is key to making the system work effectively and efficiently.[21]

Little is known about the return per dollar for the various WIA services. One nonexperimental evaluation of the WIA adult program, designed to isolate the impact of the intervention, but not using a random assignment control group, sought to distinguish the results for participants receiving core and intensive services from those receiving training services.[22] The study analyzed the difference in average earnings gains attributable to WIA program participants, with initial earnings rising $550 for women and about $700 for men. However, these increments were short term in duration and eventually declined significantly to $200 for women and between $200 and $300 for men. These modest, uncertain results for the group of participants who entered WIA programs in twelve states between June 2003 and June 2005 led the report to conclude:

> The short-term effects are greatest for individuals who do not receive training services, although the benefits that accrue to them tend to degrade over time.
>
> ...
>
> Results for WIA Adult participants who do not receive training are highly uncertain, although it is reasonable to infer that program impacts are likely to be no more than $100 or $200 per quarter [per person in earnings] over the four years following program entry.

However, for participants in expensive training programs, the report concluded:

> Those who obtained training services have lower initial returns, but they catch up to others within ten quarters, ultimately registering larger total gains.
>
> ...
>
> At the same time, WIA training impacts could be substantially greater [than the non-training impacts]. By quarter 10, credible impact estimates suggest benefits of over $400 per quarter [per person in earnings]. It is also important to point out, however, that such an estimate is an average, and differences across states may be large.

However, one expert has sounded a cautionary note with respect to job training programs generally:

> Since there is little evidence of jobs being newly created for the graduates of training programs, it seems likely that programs indeed serve a purely distributional function. To the extent that this is true, all of the earnings gains provided by all jobs training programs are illusory.[23]

A lack of accountability pervades One-Stop services according to another expert:

> ...One-Stops are only held accountable for meeting intensive service goals. They rarely have accurate counts of clients receiving core services, and they fail to take cost into account, even though intensive services cost about a hundred times more per person than core services. I estimate that 20 percent or more of staff time is wasted on tasks with little or no value, such as monitoring job searches of clients no longer receiving services. In addition, I estimate that 20 percent or more funds are wasted because One-Stops too often use expensive services when low-cost services would be equally effective.[24]

Finally, studies indicate that many WIBs have not implemented a sound partnership with other institutions to integrate and coordinate a broad range of services for individuals and businesses.[25] Although the WIA sought to consider business as the key customer of the workforce development system, this change has often not been implemented, despite more than a decade of experience. Administrators continue to focus on job seekers in the One-Stop Centers' core services using a traditional social service approach. As a result, businesses, both as customers and managers participating in system oversight, have not become involved as effective members of many local WIBs. A need thus exists for WIBs, particularly local boards, to better link employers and service providers, so as to better coordinate the training and placement of individuals to the demand side of the labor market. Greater effectiveness may require the consolidation of local WIBs or the coordination of services to meet metropolitan or regional needs. In addition to the adult program and youth activities, the WIA also funds the Job Corps.

Job Corps

The Job Corps provides academic and vocational training for eligible youth in more than 120 (123) centers throughout the United States for up to two years.[26] The centers may be operated by a federal, state, or local agency, an area vocational school, a residential vocational school, or a private entity. The program serves low-income youth ages sixteen to twenty-one (with up to 20 percent of the enrollees, ages twenty-two to twenty-four) with one or more specified characteristics, including a basic skills deficiency, a school dropout, a parent, an individual who requires additional education, vocational training, or intensive counseling and related assistance to participate in regular schoolwork or to secure and hold employment.

It is a full-time, year-round, largely residential program where the youth divide their time between the classroom instruction toward the achievement of their General Educational Development (GED) or a high school diploma and career training focused on the acquisition of a technical skill. At a center, students receive academic, vocational, employment, and social skills training, work-based learning (vocational skills training and on-the-job training), counseling and other support services, and monthly allowances for clothing and living expenses. As the nation's largest federally funded training program for at-risk youth, it strives to help eligible participants gain academic and technical competence in a career field. In addition to career preparation, it seeks to provide career development, for example, job search skills, and helps youths obtain a job.

The Job Corps serves more than 60,000 new participants each year at an annual cost of some $1.7 billion ($1,708 billion in fiscal years 2010 and 2011), or about 60 percent of all funds spent by the Department of Labor on youth training and employment services. It is an expansive program, with an annual cost of about $28,000 per participant.

For all the billions of dollars spent on the program over the years, empirical studies show mixed results, with the most recent studies finding that the Job Corps had no positive impact on participants, calling "into question" ... "the notion that Job Corps represents an effective intervention for out-of-school, disadvantaged youth in the long run."[27] The final report, using official government data, concluded that benefits to society from the Job Corps (excluding a reduction in future criminal activities) were smaller than the program's costs. The study placed the per participant costs ($13,844) to society in excess of benefits ($3,695) at some $10,200 ($10,150).[28] It also found that the program had no impact on participants' medium- and long-term earnings or moving them to full-time employment.[29] The study also mentioned that there was no evidence that suggested that this lack of earnings or employment impact would persist over time. The earnings impact for the sixteen- to nineteen-year-olds when the data were collected could potentially increase as they mature into their late twenties or early thirties and begin to experience the full benefits of Job Corps participation. However, in addition to a decrease in the receipt of public assistance and the use of substance abuse treatment programs, the Job Corps generated benefits against recidivism by reducing arrest and conviction rates. About 33 percent and 25 percent of the control group members were arrested and convicted, respectively, during the forty-eight-month follow-up period compared to 29 percent and 22 percent, respectively, of the program group members.[30] The Job Corps also generated other benefits, including modest changes in self-perceived health status.

YouthBuild

The federally funded YouthBuild program provides eligible youth with work experience while they build or rehabilitate housing in their communities for low-income or homeless individuals and families.[31] Every housing unit that a YouthBuild-funded project constructs or rehabilitates must be available for rental by or sale to low-income families or for use as transitional or permanent housing to assist homeless individuals achieve independent living.

At a cost of $80 million in fiscal year 2011, a $22.5 million drop from the $102.5 million in fiscal year 2010 funding, the program combines job training and education services. It operates at some 225 (226) sites across the United States. Each nonresidential site has from 15 to 300 participants, with the program serving about 8,000 young adults annually.

Youths are eligible to participate in the programs if they are (1) between ages sixteen to twenty-four; (2) a member of, among other groups, a low-income family, an ex-offender, or a child of an incarcerated parent; and (3) a school dropout. Youths who do not meet the disadvantaged or education criteria may be eligible, if they are basic skills deficient (despite having earned a high school diploma or GED) or have been referred by a high school for the purpose of obtaining a high school diploma or GED certificate. Typically, 90 percent of the participants have left high school without a diploma and about one-third (36 percent) have been court involved.

The young adults split their time between a construction site, where they engage in workforce development activities, including skill building, and the classroom, where they earn their GED or a high school diploma. The educational aspect of the program typically takes place in alternative schools with small class sizes that emphasize on individualized instruction. Thus, every program is functionally a school and a job training experience. Some YouthBuild-funded programs, such as Improved Solutions for Urban Schools, discussed in Chapter 4, are charter schools.

Participants stay in the program from six to twenty-four months, with an average stay of between nine and eleven months. During their time in the program, they typically alternate weeks between being full-time students and full-time participants in job training activities. They also take part in counseling, peer support groups, and life-planning exercises designed to encourage them to overcome negative habits and pursue positive life goals.

Evaluations of the program show mixed results. The housing construction or rehabilitation part of the program enables youth to learn important general job skills and specific trade skills. Generally speaking, however, the training process is slow. As a result, each site completes only a very small number of projects, typically, one to two, per year.[32] Thus, the YouthBuild program makes only a limited contribution to expanding the supply of permanent, affordable housing for homeless individuals and low-income families using disadvantaged youths' labor. Also, because the housing construction component represents a key part of YouthBuild, it is appropriate to include the cost of this component as part of the total program costs, thereby substantially increasing the cost per participant.

Although numerous studies exist with respect to the impact of the YouthBuild program, none of the thirty-two studies published or released between 1996 and 2009 used the "gold standard" experimental design, which involves comparing a participant group with a randomly assigned, similar control group.[33] In terms of educational attainment, YouthBuild participants came up significantly short compared to those in the Job Corps program. About 29 percent of a group of participants who entered YouthBuild lacking a high school credential succeeded in obtaining a diploma or GED while participating in the program or immediately after graduation. Forty-seven percent of a group of Job Corps participants attained the credential during a similar timeframe.[34]

With respect to desistance from crime, using a quasi-experimental approach, one study found that the two-year postprogram recidivism rate among a group of YouthBuild members in an incarcerated youth reentry program was 3.4–9 percent lower than a purported, similar youth cohort group.[35] While using methodological techniques to minimize the differences between the intervention and the comparison groups that could impact on the outcomes measured, the two groups in the study were not, however, formed by random assignment.

In terms of the impact of the YouthBuild program on subsequent employment, the GAO noted a lack of consistently recorded data on the YouthBuild programs.[36] This lack of data has resulted in an inability to track performance outcomes, for example, postprogram construction employment obtained and retained.

Federal Tax and Other Financial Incentives

In addition to funding various programs under the WIA, the federal government offers various financial incentives, including tax credits, to employers who hire new employees who qualify as members of disadvantaged groups, including ex-offenders. This section analyzes the Work Opportunity Tax Credit, the EZEC, and the Federal Bonding Program.

Work Opportunity Tax Credit

Employers receive a federal Work Opportunity Tax Credit[37] for hiring eligible workers, who as presently structured, began work for an employer prior to January 1, 2012 (January 1, 2013 for qualified veterans). The credit equals 40 percent of the first $6,000 of an individual's wages attributable to services rendered during a worker's first year of employment, provided he or she performs 400 or more hours of service for the employer. In other words, the maximum credit generally equals $2,400. The wage limitation is increased for certain qualified veterans. The percentage is reduced to 25 percent for individuals who perform at least 120 hours but less than 400 hours of service at the firm during the one-year period beginning on the day the employee begins work for the employer. The percentage is zero if the individual performs less than 120 hours of service during that period.

The new employees must be members of a targeted group, such as designated community residents and qualified ex-felons.[38] A designated community resident must meet two conditions. First, the individual must have attained age eighteen but not age forty on the hiring date. Second, he or she must reside within an empowerment zone, enterprise community, or renewal community. In brief, areas across the United States have been classified as empowerment zones, by the federal government, or enterprise zones, by state governments, to provide incentives for companies to invest in these designated areas. The U.S. Department of Housing and Urban Development designates renewal communities targeted for renewal that have been nominated by state and local governments. A qualified ex-felon must meet two conditions. He or she must have been convicted of a felony under a federal or state statute, and be hired not more than one year after the last date on which he or she was convicted or released from prison. Eligible employees must be certified by a designated local agency for their employer to take the credit.

Employers receive the tax credit just once per employee; not every year an individual remains employed. In other words, there is no tax incentive for employer to keep an employee after it receives the tax credit. Furthermore, no guarantee exists as to the quality of jobs the individuals receive.

The credit has not achieved much for targeted group members. Being labeled a targeted group member may be harmful to low-skilled, hard-to-employ individuals. This may account for one study's estimate that the participation rate for eligible disadvantaged youth, then a targeted group, equaled less than 17 percent.[39] Targeted group members who were hired generally exhibited the high turnover rates typical of low-wage workers.[40] For program participants, the credit likely had no positive impact on their long-term employment.[41]

The U.S. Employment Service, in consultation with the Internal Revenue Service, must take necessary and appropriate steps to keep employers informed about the availability of the credit.[42] However, many employers may be unaware of their ability to claim the credit.[43] Even if they are aware of the credit, it is not attractive to employers.

Employer use of the credit is low, resulting from both a lack of knowledge about the program and a desire to avoid the headaches often associated with hiring "risky" employees. (The employer perception of hiring ex-felons was discussed in Chapter 1.)

Large corporations, that is, those with $1 billion or more in total revenues typically account for most of the firms using the Work Opportunity Tax Credit. For example, these corporations accounted for about $177 million or 80 percent of this credit in 1999.[44] These larger businesses were more likely to know about the credit, and their substantial hiring needs made it financially beneficial to learn about and develop procedures to use the credit. Other employers may, however, have an inaccurate perception of the required paperwork. This can be remedied by hiring consultants and intermediaries to help with the paperwork in return for a share of the credit. However, because of the short job tenure pattern, resulting from the nature of low-wage, high turnover work, an average employer's return may be too low to justify its participation.[45] Employees may not be employed long enough to qualify for the 40 percent credit, with very few qualifying their employers for the maximum credit of $2,400. Thus, the credit likely offsets less than one-half of the cost of recruiting, hiring, and training credit-eligible workers.[46]

Even if used by employers, the credit may not generate any new employment. One study found that the employers surveyed would have hired members of the targeted group even if credit were not available,[47] thereby suggesting that the credit essentially serves as a windfall to employers who would anyway have hired the same employees.

Empowerment Zone Employment Tax Credit

The Internal Revenue Code also allows employers to claim an EZEC for tax-qualified zone wages.[48] The 20 percent credit applies each year to the first $15,000 of zone wages for each employee. A qualified zone employee must meet three conditions: (1) perform substantially all of his or her required services for the employer within the empowerment zone in the employer's business, (2) reside in the empowerment zone while performing the services, and (3) not be an ineligible employee. No limits exist on the number of qualified employees who can work for an employer. Furthermore, wages taken into account for the Work Opportunity Tax Credit cannot be used to qualify for the EZEC, with the $15,000 cap reduced by any wages taken into account in computing the Work Opportunity Tax Credit.

Little data exists on the use of EZEC tax credit, among other credits.[49] Businesses cite several reasons for not taking advantage of this tax benefit, including not knowing about it and finding the calculations too complicated.[50] Small firms and start-up business, having no federal tax liabilities, also find tax credits of no benefit.

Federal Bonding Program

The longstanding Federal Bonding Program, developed in 1966 by the Department of Labor, strives to encourage the hiring of ex-offenders, among others.[51] The program seeks to lessen the burden on employers by providing them with bonding insurance for new employees deemed "risky," including people with a record of arrest, conviction, or imprisonment, and anyone on probation or having a police record, who otherwise would be denied coverage by commercial insurers. Employers can be reimbursed for $5,000–$25,000 for losses resulting from theft, forgery, larceny, or embezzlement perpetrated by "risky" employees. In short, the program tries to alleviate employers' concerns that individuals with criminal records, among others, would be untrustworthy employees, by allowing employers to purchase fidelity bonds to indemnify them for the loss of money or property sustained through their employees' dishonest acts.

Employers pay nothing for $5,000 of coverage for the first six months after a "risky" employee's job start date and can purchase up to $20,000 of additional coverage. The bond insurance is for all jobs, private or public, full- or part-time, but does not cover liabilities resulting from other causes, such as poor workmanship, job injuries, or work accidents.

Employer interest in the bonds is limited. About 2,000 bonds per year were issued in the late 1970s and early 1980s. Fewer than 1,000 per year were sold in the first years of the first decade of this century.[52] In addition to employers' lack of information regarding the program,[53] the amount of bonding coverage is inadequate, whether $5,000 or up to $25,000, likely not covering any losses if they occur. Furthermore, six months may be an insufficient time period to determine an employee's trustworthiness.

In sum, the Federal Bonding Program, together with the Work Opportunity Tax Credit and the EZEC, offers inadequate rewards to motivate most employers to hire the disconnected and ex-offenders,[54] thereby casting doubt on the effectiveness of these strategies for improving the employment prospects of so-called "risky" employees.

Current Federal Programs Targeting Offenders and the Formerly Incarcerated

Today, various programs seek to make rehabilitation, rather than punishment, a central goal of the federal criminal justice system, particularly for ex-prisoners reentering society.[55] Reformers sought to refocus prerelease prison programs to emphasize preparation for employment on the outside and deal with a variety of complex challenges, including housing and family issues that complicate reentry. Also prerelease programs, they asserted, ought to establish connections to required postrelease mental health providers and substance abuse treatment, whether inpatient and/or outpatient. In general, by pursuing a comprehensive approach that links prison-based services to community-based programs on release from prison, reentry-focused agencies and organizations ought to partner with families, employers, local residents, and community groups to create circles of support for ex-inmates, thereby dissuading them from returning to crime. Reflecting a desire to facilitate cooperation among providers, reformers hoped that the postincarceration services would be delivered through the collaboration of the criminal justice, public health, and social service systems.

This section provides an overview of current federal reentry efforts. It discusses the SCA of 2008 that provides federally funded grants for various reentry programs. Also considered are the efforts of the BOP, a competitive grants program administered by the Department of Labor, and a grants program offered by the Department of Education. State and local reentry efforts targeted at offenders and those with criminal convictions are beyond the scope of this book.

Second Chance Act

The SCA[56] provides federal funding for various demonstration and other programs to assist prisoners in returning successfully to society. One of the act's stated purposes was "to build upon the innovative and successful State reentry programs developed under the [Serious and Violent Offender Reentry Initiative] (SVORI)...,"[57] an interagency pilot program that supported a range of jurisdictions and programs tackling the reentry dilemma through grants and technical assistance.[58] In brief, the SVORI funded some sixty-nine agencies that developed programs having criminal justice, employment, education, health, and housing components for released prisoners. Before and after release, program participants were provided education and training as well as family, health, and other transitional services.

A rigorous evaluation, released in 2009 after the enactment of the SCA in 2008, assessed the impact of the SVORI on participants at twelve adult and four juvenile sites.[59] The mixed findings with respect to adult males is of particular interest. For adult males, participation somewhat lowered arrest rates three to twenty-four months after release compared to nonparticipants, but these differences were not statically significant. Reincarceration rates of adult male participants were statistically indistinguishable from the reincarceration rates of nonparticipants throughout the twenty-four months postrelease; however, the rates were higher for participants after three months. Adult male participants enjoyed moderately better postrelease employment experiences than nonparticipants. They were more likely to be supporting themselves with a job three and fifteen months postrelease and appeared to have secured better jobs that provided formal pay and benefits. However, legislators did not have the benefit of these mixed results when they passed the SCA.

As an initial step to alleviate the prisoner reentry problem, the SCA authorized up to $330 million in federal funding during fiscal years 2009 and 2010, with grants going to state and local governments as well as nongovernmental groups to implement four types of prisoner reentry programs. First, the SCA funds improvements to existing programs, namely, the reauthorization of adult and juvenile state and local reentry demonstration projects and the improvement of the residential substance abuse treatment for state offenders. Second, the act funds new and innovative programs to improve offender reentry services, including grants for family-based substance abuse treatment, grants to evaluate and improve education at prisons, jails, and juvenile facilities, and technology careers training demonstration grants. Third, the SCA funds enhanced drug treatment programs through the offender reentry substance abuse and criminal justice collaboration program. Fourth, the act establishes a grants program for nonprofit organizations to provide mentoring and other transitional services essential to reintegrating both adult and juvenile ex-offenders into the community. (The benefits of mentoring are discussed in Chapters 3 and 4.) To date, the impact of these grants to public sector and nonprofit pilot programs and demonstration projects has not been evaluated.

Also funded by the act, the Department of Justice Second Chance Act Offender Reentry Initiative seeks to facilitate inmates' reintegration into society by funding demonstration grants. The act further directs units of the justice department, namely, the National Institute of Justice and the Bureau of Justice Statistics, to increase research on reentry issues.

The act also imposes new requirements on the BOP to facilitate the successful reentry of federal inmates into their communities and reduce the recidivism rate. Through the Federal Prisoner Reentry Initiative, the act requires the identifying, tracking, addressing, and reporting on inmate skills needs and provides incentives for prisoner participation in skills development programs.

Federal Bureau of Prisons

BOP is the largest correctional system in the United States. The BOP is responsible for about 211,000 (211,686) inmates. BOP's reentry programs, including its residential reentry housing centers, receive substantial federal funding. In fiscal year 2011, Congress funded BOP's reentry programs at about $564 million.

The federal prison system has traditionally offered an extensive array of programs to prepare inmates for release and reduce recidivism. Today, it provides extensive educational and job training programs. All of its institutions offer literacy classes. Inmates who do not have a high school diploma or a GED must participate in the literacy program for at least 240 hours or until they obtain their GED. Occupational and vocational training programs are also offered in a number of areas.[60]

However, whether because of inmate disinterest or program capacity problems, only a limited percentage of inmates in federal prisons receive educational programming. In 2004, the percentage of federal inmates who received educational and job training programs postadmission equaled 21 percent for adult secondary education, 31 percent for vocational training, and 29 percent for life skills.[61] Because the categories are not mutually exclusive, an inmate, for example, may receive both adult secondary education and vocational training.

An important component in federal correctional institutions is on-the-job training through institutional job assignments and employment in UNICOR Federal Prison Industries, Inc. (FPI), a wholly owned U.S. government income-producing business that sells goods and services to the federal government.[62] All inmates who are physically and mentally able must perform work that contributes to an institution's operation.[63] Thus, in 1997, 87 percent of all federal inmates had work assignments, typically institutional maintenance tasks that keep prisons running, but only 17 percent of all federal inmates had assignments with the FPI.[64] By fiscal year 2010, inmates who performed services for FPI constituted only about 9 percent of work-eligible participants.[65]

Over the years, the BOP failed to meet its inmate completion goals for its occupational and vocational training programs and on-the-job projects. For example, during the period from fiscal year 1999 through fiscal year 2002, 38–64 percent of the federal incarceration institutions failed to meet their inmate occupational completion goals.[66] Furthermore, the BOP lacked a mechanism to hold its institutions accountable for meeting their respective goals and facilities were not required to develop or implement corrective action plans to remedy performance failures and ensure that goals would be met in the future.

Despite these programmatic deficiencies, research has shown that inmates who participated in the BOP's work and jobs skills efforts were substantially less likely to recidivate. The Post-Release Employment Project (PREP) compared inmates who worked at the FPI and/or who received vocational and apprentice training with those who did not participate.[67] The PREP study found that those who participated were 35 percent less likely to have their parole revoked, 6.6 percent of the intervention group versus 10.1 percent for the comparison group, twelve months postrelease. The participants were 14 percent more likely to be employed than the group of statistically similar inmates who did not participate by the twelfth month following release, 71.7 percent versus 63.1 percent. The study found that the benefits of participation carried over the long term, even as many as eight to twelve years postrelease. Inmates who worked for FPI were 24 percent less likely to recidivate than nonparticipants during the eight- to twelve-year follow-up period. Those who participated in either vocational or apprenticeship training were 33 percent less likely to recidivate during that period.

The BOP empirical data on work programs and vocational training accords with metaanalyses and systematic research reviews on the positive impact of in-prison vocational educational programs, although these other studies show less beneficial results. One metaanalysis concluded that prisoners who participated in vocational education programs while incarcerated had a 12.6 percent lower likelihood of recidivism.[68] These vocational educational programs cost about $2,000 per participant and saved about $12,000 in criminal justice expenditures per participant. Furthermore, research indicated that state in-prison correctional industries programs reduced recidivism by 7.8 percent.[69]

In previous years, the BOP traditionally used an unstructured case management assessment for each inmate and a competency-based model with success measured by skill acquisition, not by program completion and reentry success factors, such as rates of employment and recidivism. Then, in June 2003, BOP established the Inmate Skills Development branch within its Correctional Programs Division. It was first charged with the development of a comprehensive inmate skills assessment process. It was also charged with the coordination of BOP programs and their linkage to address skill needs.

This effort evolved into the Inmate Skills Development Initiative (ISDI) that represents a shift in strategic emphasis by the BOP and a new way of viewing inmates, their management, and their preparation for release.[70] The BOP identified nine skills as significantly impacting on an offender's successful transition back to society. Through an Inmate Skills Assessment (ISA), the BOP staff expects to receive a comprehensive picture of each inmate's strengths and weaknesses with respect to release readiness. The skill baseline helps maximize programming opportunities and more efficiently targets resource allocations. From the information obtained through an ISA, the BOP staff develops a comprehensive Inmate Skills Development Plan for each inmate. In collaboration with BOP staff, each inmate sets goals to remediate deficiencies, with reentry skill development linked to BOP programs. Progress is monitored with respect to skill acquisition on an individual basis through regular reviews. In sum, through the ISDI, the Bureau of Prisons intends to assess inmate skills levels and measure skills inmates acquire through its reentry programs, with the ultimate goal of reducing recidivism.

The GAO found that BOP had mechanisms in place to address most (nine of twelve) of the SCA's requirements imposed on the federal prison system, but it may not have done all that is needed to implement a requirement or that it did so effectively.[71] The BOP is working to implement the ISDI to meet the remaining requirements; however, these requirements will not be met until 2014, at the earliest. Furthermore, the BOP had not fully developed a detailed ISDI implementation plan, thereby rendering it difficult for the GAO to assess BOP's progress toward realizing the ISDI's objectives and identifying the ISDI's impact on the successful reentry of ex-offenders into their communities.

Reintegration of Ex-Offenders

The WIA and the SCA fund a competitive grants program, Reintegration of Ex-Offenders, administered by the Department of Labor.[72] The program includes both Prisoner Reentry Initiative grants for programs serving adult returning offenders and Youth Offender grants focused on at-risk youth aged fourteen to twenty-one, who have been involved with or have a high risk of involvement in gangs or the juvenile justice system or who attend "persistently dangerous" schools. Seeking to increase employment, job retention, and earnings of releasees and decrease recidivism, the adult returning offenders program, annually is designed to strengthen urban communities through an employment-centered program for adults, age eighteen and older, incorporating mentoring, job training, and other transitional services, such as housing. Faith-based and community organizations play a key role in this initiative by providing job training and placement, making referrals to the One-Stop system, connecting with providers of occupational skills training, and providing or referring the formerly incarcerated to needed support services, such as substance abuse treatment. Educational services and hard skills training are provided by organizations that grant industry-recognized credentials. Participating ex-offenders are matched with appropriate mentors who are primarily responsible for supporting the returnees in the community and the workplace. As discussed further in Chapter 3, mentors offer support, guidance, and assistance with the challenges ex-offenders face.

The grants for youthful offenders program strive to prevent in-school youth from dropping out of school through alternative education and related services. The program also seeks to increase the employment rate of out-of-school youth, enhance youth reading and math skills, reduce the involvement of youth in crime and violence, and decrease youth recidivism.

Workplace and Community Transition for Inmates

The Department of Education offers grants to the states that are used for workplace and community transition training for incarcerated individuals.[73] Eligible individuals must have already earned a high school diploma or a GED, and must be (1) eligible to be released (or paroled) within seven years, (2) age thirty-five or younger, and (3) not convicted of certain offenses. The program seeks to assist and encourage eligible incarcerated individuals to acquire educational and job skills through coursework to prepare them to pursue postsecondary education while in prison or employment counseling, among other services, during incarceration and before the end of two years postincarceration.

Evaluating Current Federal Workforce Development Programs

Two points are noteworthy in evaluating the existing federal workforce development programs: first, the massive duplication of efforts; and, second, the need for rigorous assessment of programmatic effectiveness. Federal expenditures on employment and training are scattered among many agencies with overlapping agendas. Even an ardent proponent of ever-increasing funding for federal workforce development programs admitted in an understatement, "No doubt, there is some waste, duplication, and a lack of coordination in such a situation."[74]

Illustrative of the programmatic duplication, a recent study by the GAO found forty-seven separate federally funded employment and training programs, designed to help job seekers obtain employment.[75] Three major programs out of the forty-seven exist, namely, the Employment Service, which provides core services at the One-Stop Centers to adult job seekers, particularly unemployment insurance claimants, and the WIA adult program, both administered by the Department of Labor, as well as the Temporary Assistance for Needy Families program, administered by the Department of Health and Human Services. According to the GAO, these programs often provide some of the same services to the same population but through separate administrative structures. The other forty-four out of the forty-seven programs overlap with at least one other program providing at least one similar service to a similar population group.

The bottom line: given the extent of duplication, programs with similar goals, target populations, and services must be coordinated, consolidated, or streamlined across federal agencies, so that goals are consistent and program efforts mutually reinforcing. For example, within the WIA's existing WIB structure, the Departments of Labor, Education, and Commerce, among others, must come together and establish common goals for state and local WIBs so individuals and businesses receive more integrated services. State agencies and federal departments providing funding and issuing regulations for the WIBs must be better aligned. No longer can the public sector work at cross-purposes and create silos with conflicting regulations. The WIA governance mechanism and funding structure must be horizontally coordinated among all public sector levels.[76]

Also, a need exists for the rigorous, independent assessment of federally funded workforce development and prisoner reentry programs. We need to know what works in each program as a whole and in its various parts, so that federal agencies can modify (or even abandon) programs that are not working. In short, funding consequences must attach for programmatic results, particularly in terms of costs and benefits.

The more rigorous the research methodology used, the more confident we can be in the validity of an evaluation's findings. Wherever possible, an evaluation ought to use random assignment approach, the most reliable evidence-based method available.[77] Of course, some programs are not suitable for random evaluation. They may be too small or they accept all applicants and thus cannot create a control group. In these cases, a need exists for a credible evaluation alternative. However, it is preferable to use the "gold standard" method that randomly assigns participants to either an intervention group, whose members take part in a program, or a control group, whose members do not participate in a program. If properly conducted, using large samples, random assignment experiments achieve a high degree of causal validity. The similarity of the intervention and control groups means that the two groups are likely to be exposed to the same outside forces, thereby ruling out other causes, such as preintervention variations between the two groups, and to respond to those forces in similar ways. Any subsequent differences in average outcomes between the two groups can be attributed to program, to a known degree of statistical precision.

In addition to the experimental evaluation of effectiveness with control groups, wherever possible, enactment legislation and funding authorization ought to stipulate specific monitoring requirements, including nationwide, multisite experimental evaluations. Legislation should require independent organizations to perform these evaluations in a timely manner and impose funding and other penalties on departments and agencies that fail to meet the timeliness mandate.

In testing for differences between the randomly assigned intervention and control groups, the evidence-based approach will help hold programs accountable for results. It will point the way to which programs to support and at what funding levels, recognizing that programmatic and funding decisions also reflect cultural values and political realities.

Under a tiered funding approach, for example, the largest grant awards in a federally funded program would go to proven interventions.[78] Other grants would fund interventions supported by moderately or preliminarily positive evidence on the condition that they be subject to rigorous evaluation. If found effective, they would be eligible for top-tier funding; if not, funds would be directed to other, hopefully more promising interventions.

As a step to improving the effectiveness of federal social service programs, in its 2012 budget, the Obama administration sought to implement a pilot program for performance-based awards.[79] Seemingly, the program will use social impact bonds as the funding mechanisms, with the aim of facilitating more productive, but less costly, programs.

Social impact bonds enlist investors, initially foundations and ultimately for-profit entities, to put up funds to run social service programs that the federal government normally pays for. Social impact bonds represent a "pay for success" funding technique. If investors back a program that achieves results and meets performance goals in comparison to a control group that is not part of the program, the federal government will reimburse them plus provide a bonus. If the program fails to meet its benchmarks, the government will not repay the investors.

The plan has three benefits. First, funds are directed to programs achieving results. If the performance goals are not met, the federal government pays nothing, thereby encouraging the growth of effective, results-oriented social service programs. This approach enables the federal government to better monitor the success of nonprofit organizations providing social services. Second, foundations will invest their endowments in the bonds and achieve a good return while helping alleviate social problems. Funders will hopefully get their money back and use it again. Social impact bonds may also attract for-profit investors, thereby expanding the pool of capital for social service programs. Third, if successful, the approach will reduce the fundraising headaches for nonprofit organizations running programs.

The goal of bringing more marketplace discipline to social service programs by improving their performance is, of course, laudable. However, coming up with performance measures and obtaining agreement on these benchmarks may be difficult. It is unclear, at present, who will set the performance standards and, even more importantly, who will judge whether they have been met. In the end, investors, whether foundations or for-profit entities, may only gravitate to supporting easy-to-document programs, while foregoing complex programs, requiring a multiplicity of efforts, such as those directed at disconnected persons and ex-offenders.

Looking back over this chapter's survey of federally funded workforce development and reentry programs for the disconnected and for those with criminal convictions, as is the case for the public sector expenditures more generally, a need exists for improved efficiency (and productivity) and for greater accountability for achieving results. Funding agencies must also strengthen the accountability and performance of nonprofit organizations receiving federal monies to improve their programmatic effectiveness. Admittedly, however, these are difficult tasks.

Public sector service providers and funders must develop and implement goal-oriented strategic plans and metrics to measure the effectiveness of each dollar spent. Metrics—the quantitative definition of desired outcomes—are needed to measure whether programs are achieving the desired outcomes. Expecting results and achieving accountability, policymakers must create a sound path to produce the desired outcomes and then measure, through rigorous evaluations designed to assess theoretical frameworks, the outcomes achieved for each dollar expended. Through the measurement of program effectiveness, that is, the ratio of costs to various outcomes, we can identify less successful (or ineffective) programs ripe for elimination, consolidation, coordination, or reduction in size. Programs may need to provide desired social services in a completely restructured manner. Spurring an effectiveness approach will help Congress and federal departments and agencies make sound budgetary choices in an era of fiscal responsibility.

In any event, a cautionary note is in order. Effective programs, particularly for ex-inmates, turn, in large measure, on each individual's resolve to change one's life. As two experts concluded:

> ...[T]he overwhelming evidence from thirty years and billions of dollars of government spending is that it is very difficult to change an individual's employment status and earnings level and therefore their crime participation, especially for those individuals most embedded in criminal activity. We believe the primary reason is that they themselves need to be motivated to work before things like job skills can make a difference; although

unemployment may have contributed to their criminal activity, a job opportunity (and job skill training) by itself does not solve the problem.[80]

Public Sector Fiscal Realities

Today, fiscal reality has forced a limit on the size and ambitions of all levels of government. Reckless, unsustainable spending has resulted in public sector fiscal austerity, now and for the foreseeable future.

On the federal level, massive trillion-dollar deficits, with a $1.3 trillion deficit projected for fiscal year 2011, exist as far as the eye can see. Both the Congressional Budget Office and the GAO have warned that the trajectory of the federal budget and the accompanying deficits cannot be sustained.[81]

The gap between revenues and spending at nearly 9 percent of the U.S. Gross Domestic Product (GDP) led to a growing publicly held federal debt burden of 62 percent of GDP in 2010; with the gross federal debt equal to nearly 92 percent of GDP.[82] Unless steps are taken, the publicly held debt burden may reach an unsustainable 100 percent of GDP in another decade. The necessary fiscal constraints place limits on what the federal government can do with respect to workforce development and prison reentry programs and, more generally, social service programs. If the massive deficits continue over the next decade, the future interest payments on the debt will likely stifle the American economy. To deal with these fiscal problems, given the unlikelihood of raising taxes or trimming big entitlement programs, such as Medicare and Social Security, at least in the near term, the federal government will likely downsize its funding of domestic social service programs, as part of an effectiveness revolution.

State and local governments are also in dire fiscal straits.[83] States are looking at an aggregate of some $130 billion in budgetary short-falls in 2011. States and localities also face some trillion dollars in unfunded liabilities for pension and health care benefits promised retirees. To balance their budgets and in response to the end of federal stimulus funds, states closed the revenue gap by increasing taxes and implementing severe spending reductions that involved slashing social service programs as well as decreasing aid provided to local governments. In turn, localities cut expenditures. Although state revenues are improving, they remain below the levels prior to the Great Recession.

The bottom line: the American public appears to be coming to grips with the public sector's financial recklessness. The ever-increasing public expenditure route of the past fifty years is unsustainable. As former Chicago mayor Richard M. Daley put it, "The idea that we come down to Washington, and they have all this money, it's wrong. Those days are over."[84]

Public sector fiscal responsibility will likely lead to increased reliance on nonprofit organizations and social entrepreneurs to help meet America's workforce development needs for disconnected individuals and ex-offenders. As a result of the Great Recession, many nonprofits have experienced financial struggles in an era of diminished donations. Hopefully, foundations, corporations, and wealthy individuals will step up their funding of effective nonprofit organizations, with the public sector continuing to provide some level of financial support together with oversight and increased accountability. With economic pressures easing, the uptick in charitable giving in 2010, after two years of steep declines, offers a hopeful sign.[85] Effective community-based nonprofit programs can help meet the rehabilitative challenges presented by the disconnected and ex-offenders.

Notes

1. Heather C. West and others, "Prisoners in 2009," U.S. Department of Justice, Office of Justice Programs, Bureau of Justice Statistics, December 2010, NCJ 231675, 4 (Table 2 Number of sentenced prisoners admitted into and released from state and federal jurisdictions, 2000–2009).

2. Patrick A. Langan and David J. Levin, "Recidivism of Prisoners Released in 1994," U.S. Department of Justice, Office of Justice Programs, Bureau of Justice Statistics, June 2002, NCJ 193427, 1, 3, 7. For a summary of recidivism statistics see Blas Nuñez-Neto, "Offender Reentry: Correctional Statistics, Reintegration into the Community, and Recidivism," Congressional Research Service, July 11, 2008, PL34287, CRS-10 to CR5-14. In the first state-by-state survey of recidivism, 45.4 percent and 43.3 percent of the inmates released from prison in 1999 and 2004, respectively, were reincarcerated within three years, either for committing a new crime or for parole violations, Pew Center on the States, "State of Recidivism: The Revolving Door of America's Prisons," April 2011, 2, 9. For differences between the Pew and Bureau of Justice surveys see Ibid., 34–36.

3. Langan and Levin, "Recidivism," 3.

4. Ibid., 7.

5. For background on the dimensions of desistance from crime see National Research Council, *Parole, Desistance from Crime, and Community Integration* (Washington, DC: National Academies, 2008), 19–28. See also Christy A. Visher and Jeremy Travis, "Transitions from Prison to Community: Understanding Individual Pathways," *Annual Review of Sociology*

29 (2003): 89–113; John H. Laub and Robert J. Sampson, "Understanding Desistance from Crime," in *Crime and Justice: A Review of Research*, ed. Michael Tonry, vol. 28 (Chicago, IL: University of Chicago Press, 2001), 1–69; Paul Gendreau and others, "A Meta-Analysis of the Predictors of Adult Offender Recidivism: What Works!," *Criminology* 34, no. 4 (November 1996): 575–607.

For a summary of the impact of various factors, including employment, health, housing, substance use, and families, see Urban Institute, Justice Policy Center, "Understanding the Challenges of Prisoner Reentry: Research Findings for the Urban Institute's Prisoner Reentry Portfolio," January 2006. Joan Petersilia provided a critique of prisoner reentry principles and programs in "What Works in Prisoner Reentry? Reviewing and Questioning the Evidence," *Federal Probation* 68, no. 2 (September 2004): 4–8. See also Ricard P. Seiter and Karen R. Kadela, "Prisoner Reentry: What Works, What Doesn't, and What's Promising," *Crime and Delinquency* 49, no. 3 (July 2003): 360–88. With respect to the youth reentry process see Mercer L. Sullivan, "Youth Perspectives on the Experience of Reentry," *Youth Violence and Juvenile Justice* 2, no. 1 (January 2004): 56–71. For a summary of the "what works" programmatic literature see Nathan James, "Offender Reentry: Correctional Statistics, Reintegration into the Community, and Recidivism," Congressional Research Service, January 3, 2011, 12–14.

6. Christopher Uggen, "Work as a Turning Point in the Life Course of Criminals: A Duration Model of Age, Employment and Recidivism," *American Sociological Review* 65, no. 4 (August 2000): 529–46; Christopher Uggen and Melissa Thompson, "The Socioeconomic Determinants of Ill-Gotten Gains, Within-Person Changes in Drug Use and Illegal Earnings," *American Journal of Sociology* 109, no. 1 (July 2003): 146–85, 166, 177, 179.

7. Christopher Uggen and others, "Work and Family Perspectives on Reentry," in *Prisoner Reentry and Crime in America*, ed. Jeremy Travis and Christy Visher (New York: Cambridge University Press, 2005), 213–14.

8. Public Law 105-220. For background on the Workforce Investment Act see generally David H. Bradley, "The Workforce Investment Act and the One-Stop Delivery System," March 22, 2010, Congressional Research Service, R41135.

Burt S. Barnow and Christopher T. King, "The Workforce Investment Act in Eight States," Nelson A. Rockefeller Institute of Government, February 2005, B-1 to B-7, provided a brief historical overview of federal workforce development policies and programs. See also James Bovard, "What Job 'Training' Teaches? Bad Work Habits," *Wall Street Journal*, September 13, 2011, A17. For a summary history of federal youth employment and job training programs see Adrienne L. Fernandes-Alcantara, "Vulnerable Youth: Employment and Job Training Programs," Congressional Research Service, January 13, 2011, CRS Report R40929,4–8.

9. For background on WIA governance see Social Policy Research Associates, "The Workforce Investment Act after Five Years: Results from the National Evaluation of the Implementation of WIA," June 2004, X-1 to X-23. Kate Durham and others, "Business as Partner and Customer under WIA: A Study of Innovative Practices," June 30, 2004, II-1

to II-19, discussed business involvement with the Workforce Investment Board structure.

10. For background on the One-Stop infrastructure see Social Policy Research Associates, "Workforce Investment Act," XI-1 to XI-33. For an overview of services offered adults see Ibid., VI-1 to VI-25. Barnow and King, "Workforce Investment Act in Eight States," 22–36, 52–55, provided an evaluation of the One-Stop Centers.

11. David H. Bradley, "CRS Issue Statement on Employment and Training Policy," January 11, 2010, Congressional Research Service, IS40285, 1–3.

12. The statistics in this paragraph are from Louis S. Jacobson, "Strengthening One-Stop Centers: Helping More Unemployed Workers Find Jobs and Build Skills," Brookings Institution, The Hamilton Project, Discussion Paper 2009-01, April 2009, 6, 8–9.

13. For a summary of WIA youth activities see U.S. General Accounting Office, "Workforce Investment Act: Labor Actions Can Help States Improve Quality of Performance Outcome Data and Delivery of Youth Services," February 2004, GAO-04-308, 4–7; Social Policy Research Associates, "Workforce Investment Act," VIII-1 to VIII-17; Fernandes-Alcantara, "Vulnerable Youth," 12–19.

14. 29 USC §2871(b)(2)(A)(i). For a critique of the WIA performance management system and indicators see Barnow and King, "Workforce Investment Act," 45–48, 49–50; Dunham and others, "Business as Partner," ES-14 to ES-15, V-7.

15. 29 USC §2871(b)(2)(A)(ii). Fernandes-Alcantara, "Vulnerable Youth," 19–20, summarized the statutory and common performance measures for WIA youth programs.

16. 29 USC §2871(b)(2)(B).

17. 29 USC §2871(b)(3) and (c).

18. U.S. Office of Management and Budget, "Detailed Information on the Workforce Investment Act–Adult Employment and Training Assessment, 2005."

19. U.S. General Accounting Office, "Workforce Investment Act: Labor Actions," 30. See also Ibid., 4, 23, 26.

20. 29 USC §2917(c).

21. Statement, George A. Scott, Director, Education, Workforce, and Income Security, U.S. Government Accountability Office, Workforce Development Act: Labor Has Made Progress in Addressing Areas of Concern, but More Focus Needed on Understanding What and What Doesn't Work, Testimony Before the Subcommittee on Higher Education, Lifelong Learning, and Competitiveness, Committee on Education and Labor, House of Representatives, 111th Cong., 1st sess., February 26, 2009, GAO-09-396T, 14. See also U.S. Government Accountability Office, "Workforce Investment Act: Substantial Funds Are Used for Training, but Little is Known Nationally about Training Outcomes," June 2005, GAO-05-650, 29–31. Although states reported performance data to the Department of Labor annually, the GAO regarded such data as "questionable" because of poor state monitoring of data quality and inadequate and inconsistent state management of information systems.

22. The quotations in this paragraph are from IMPAQ International LLC, "Workforce Investment Act Non-Experimental Net Impact Evaluation,"

Final Report, December 2008, 58. See also Ibid., i–ii, 49–51. For an analysis of the overall impacts of the WIA's adult program, impact estimates for WIA core and intensive services, as well as training services see Ibid., 40–57.

23. Gordon Lafer, *The Job Training Charade* (Ithaca, NY: Cornell University Press, 2002), 116.

24. Jacobson, "Strengthening," 11–12.

25. Barnow and King, "Workforce Investment Act," vi, 14–16; Randall Eberts and George Erickcek, "The Federal Role in Helping Incumbent and Dislocated Workers Adjust to the New Economy," Metropolitan Policy Program at Brookings, September 2010, 2–3. With respect to innovative efforts to involve businesses with WIBs, see generally Dunham and others, "Business as Partner."

26. For an overview of the Job Corps see Fernandes-Alcantara, "Vulnerable Youth," 21–24.

27. Harry J. Holzer, *Workforce Development as an Antipoverty Strategy: What do We Know? What Should We Do?* (Washington, DC: Urban Institute, October 2008), 15.

28. Peter Z. Schochet and others, "National Job Corps Study: Findings Using Administrative Earnings Records Data," Mathematica Policy Research, MPR No. 8140-840, October 2003, xvi, xxviii–xxxix, 123–139, 134. In contrast, John Burghardt and others, "Does Job Corps Work?" Summary of the National Job Corps Study, Mathematica Policy Research, MPR No. 8140—530, June 2001, 5, 25–29, found the program cost-effective, with benefits to society ($31,000) exceeding costs ($14,000) by $17,000 for each participant.

29. Schochet and others, "National Job Corps Study," xvi, xix, xxi, xxvii, 142–46. In contrast, an earlier study found that the program generated positive earnings gains for participants in their third and fourth postprogram years. Burghardt and others, "Does Job Corps Work?" 15–16. It is unclear why these initial earnings gains faded after several years.

   A study of JobStart, the nonresidential version of Job Corps, not currently funded, found that the program failed to show any impact on postprogram earnings. George Cave and others, "JobStart: Final Report on a Program for School Dropouts," Manpower Demonstration Research, October 1993, xviii, xxviii, xxxi–xxxiii. Although the gains in earnings and employment were very large at one site, the Center for Employment Training (CET) in San Jose, California, these impacts were not positive at sites replicating the CET program. Cynthia Miller and others, "Working with Disadvantaged Youth: Thirty-Month Findings from the Evaluation of Employment Training Replication Sites," MDRC, June 2003. The sites replicating the CET model with high fidelity did not increase youths' employment earnings during the fifty-four-month follow-up period. The effects in medium- or low-fidelity sites were negligible or negative. Cynthia Miller and others, "The Challenge of Repeating Success in a Changing World: Final Report on the Center for Employment Training Replication Sites," MDRC, September 2005, iii, 55–56, 63–92, 99–100, 103–5.

30. John Burghardt and others, "Does Job Corps Work?" 16–18, 17 (Table 2 Impacts on Key Public Assistance and Crime Outcomes During the 48 Months after Random Assignment). See also Sheena McConnell and

Steven Glazerman, "National Job Corps Study: The Benefits and Costs of Job Corps," Mathematica Policy Research, June 2001, 72–78, 81–103. Participation in the Jobs Corps resulted in a reduction in criminal justice system processing costs and in costs to crime victims with an overall benefit of $1,240 per participant. Ibid., 81.

31. For an overview of YouthBuild see Fernandes-Alcartara, "Vulnerable Youth," 24–27.

32. Maxine V. Mitchell and others, "Evaluation of the YouthBuild Program," U.S. Department of Housing and Urban Development, Office of Policy Development and Research, Contract C-OPC-22147, August 2003, Executive Summary, n.p.

33. U.S. Department of Education, "What Works Clearinghouse, WWC Interventions Report, Dropout Prevention," YouthBuild, November 2009. Three studies of the thirty-two studies used a quasi-experimental design in which the analytical intervention and comparison groups were not shown to the equivalent (see, e.g., Mark A. Cohen and Alex R. Piquero, "Costs and Benefits of a Targeted Intervention Program for Youthful Offenders: The YouthBuild USA Offender Project," March 2008, http://ssm.com/abstract=1154055). Twenty-five studies did not use a comparison group (see, e.g., Andrew Hahn and others, "Life after YouthBuild: 900 YouthBuild Graduates Reflect on Their Lives, Dreams, and Experiences," June 2004, YouthBuild USA), with four studies out of the scope of the review for various reasons other than the study design.

34. Mitchell and others, "Evaluation," n.p. See also U.S. Government Accountability Office, "YouthBuild: Analyses of Outcome Data Needed to Determine Long-Term Benefits," February 2007, GAO-07-82, 6. In contrast, an earlier study showed that 20 percent of YouthBuild enrollees compared to 10 percent of Job Corps participants achieved their GED. Ronald F. Ferguson and Philip L. Clay, "YouthBuild in Developmental Perspective: A Formative Evaluation of the YouthBuild Demonstration Project," September 1996, 22 (Table 2A.2 In-Program Impacts for Enrollees in YouthBuild and Four Comparison Programs).

35. Cohen and Piquero, "Costs and Benefits," 8, 29–33, 54 (Table 7 Two-Year Recidivism Rate in Philadelphia Cohort Data versus Overall Recidivism Rate in YouthBuild Offender Project Sample). The study also found that the YouthBuild participants had a 23.2 percent higher high school graduation or GED rate in comparison to the National Longitudinal Survey of Youth Cohort. Ibid., 8, 33–35.

According to YouthBuild, the recidivism rate for youthful offenders who complete the program equals 5–25 percent. YouthBuild USA, "Youthful Offender Project Year 1," August 2007, 13.

For a study of the impact of the YouthBuild Offender Grants see Wally Abrazaldo and others, "Evaluation of the YouthBuild Youth Offender Grants," Final Report, May 2009, Social Policy Research Associates.

36. U.S. Government Accountability Office, "YouthBuild Program: Analysis of Outcome Data Needed to Determine Long-Term Benefits," February 2007, GAO-07-82, 5–6, 19, 24–25.

A cost-benefit study of the Minnesota YouthBuild Program concluded that the state's expenditures ($877,000) were paid off within the first year after the participants completed the program in the form of $1.5 million of direct benefits to the state ($350,000 in additional state tax revenues and $1.2 million in state prison cost savings). Minnesota Department of Economic Security, "Minnesota YouthBuild Program: A Measurement of Costs and Benefits to the State of Minnesota," Revised, February 14, 2003, 1, 8.

37. Internal Revenue Code §§38(b)(2) and §51(a). See generally, Linda Levine, "The Work Opportunity Tax Credit (WOTC) and the Welfare-to-Work (WtW) Tax Credit," CRS Report to Congress, April 27, 2005, CRS-3 to CRS-5, CRS-7.

38. Internal Revenue Code §51(g).

39. Sarah Hamersma, "The Work Opportunity and Welfare-to-Work Tax Credits: Participation Rates among Eligible Workers," *National Tax Journal* 56, no. 4 (December 2003): 725–38, at 732.

40. Westat and Decision Information Resources, Inc., "Employers' Use and Assessment of the WOTC and Welfare-to-Work Tax Credits Program," Department of Labor, Employment and Training Administration, Office of Policy and Research, March 2001, vi, 5.

41. Sarah Hamersma, "The Effects of an Employer Subsidy on Employment Outcomes: A Study of the Work Opportunity and Welfare-to-Work Tax Credits," *Journal of Policy Analysis and Management* 27, no. 3 (Summer 2008): 498–520, at 509.

42. Internal Revenue Code §51(g).

43. Jennifer Fahey and others, "Employment of Ex-Offenders: Employer Perspectives," Crime & Justice Institute, October 31, 2006, 15.

44. U.S. General Accounting Office, "Business Tax Incentives: Incentives to Employ Workers with Disabilities Receive Limited Use and Have Uncertain Impact," December 2002, GAO-03-39, 13.

45. Hamersma, "Work Opportunity," 735, 736.

46. U.S. General Accounting Office, "Work Opportunity Tax Credit: Employers do not Appear to Dismiss Employees to Increase Tax Credits," March 2001, GAO-01-329, 13–14.

47. Westat and Decision Information Resources, "Employers' Use," 9.

48. Internal Revenue Code §1396.

49. The U.S. General Accounting Office, "Community Development: Federal Revitalization Programs are being Implemented, but Data on the Use of Tax Benefits Are Limited," March 2004, GAO-04-306, 6, 30–36.

50. Ibid., 36. See also U.S. General Accounting Office, "Community Development: Businesses' Use of Empowerment Zone Tax Incentives," September 1999, GAO/RCED-99-253, 3, 10, 11 (Figure 4 Reasons for Not Claiming the Employment Credit); Scott Herbert and others, "Interim Assessment of the Empowerment Zones and Enterprise Communities (EZ/EC) Program: A Progress Report," U.S. Department of Housing and Urban Development, Office of Policy Development and Research, November 2001, 3-18 to 3-23; Letter, William B. Shear, Director, Financial Markets and Community Investment, U.S. Government Accountability Office, to Max Baucus and Sander M. Levin, March 12, 2010.

51. U.S. Department of Labor, "Federal Bonding Program," n.d.; Federal Bonding Program, Bond Package Availability and Purchase,

http://www.bond4jobs.com/bond-pkg-availability-purchase.html (accessed November 16, 2010).

52. Harry J. Holzer and others, "Employment Barriers Facing Ex-Offenders, Urban Institute Reentry Roundtable, Employment Dimensions of Reentry: Understanding the Nexus Between Prisoner Reentry and Work," May 2003, 17, fn 33.

53. Fahey and others, "Engel, Employment of Ex-Offenders," 15.

54. However, in focus groups of employers, 61 percent viewed bond incentives, at least in the abstract, as having a positive or very positive impact on hiring decisions regarding ex-offenders. In contrast, half of the participants viewed tax incentives as having little or no impact on hiring decisions. Ibid., 14.

55. Key writings that spurred the trend to rehabilitation include Jeremy Travis, *But They All Come Back: Facing the Challenges of Prisoner Reentry* (Washington, DC: Urban Institute, 2005); Joan Petersilia, *When Prisoners Come Home: Parole and Prisoner Reentry* (New York: Oxford University Press, 2003).

56. Public Law 110-119. See also Erik Eckholm, "U.S. Shifting Prison Focus to Re-Entry into Society," *New York Times*, April 8, 2008, A23.

57. 42 USC § 17501(a)(5).

58. For background on the Serious and Violent Offender Reentry Initiative that in fiscal years 2003 and 2004 awarded a total of $116.8 million in grants see U.S. Department of Justice, "Office of Inspector General, Audit Division, Office of Justice Programs' Management of Its Offender Reentry Initiative," July 2010, Audit Report 10–34, 2–4.

59. Pamela K. Lattimore and Christy A. Visher, "The Multi-Site Evaluation of SVORI: Summary and Synthesis," December 2009. vi, 81, 86–87. For females, SVORI participants in comparison to nonparticipants were less likely to be rearrested within nine to twenty-one months postrelease and to be supporting themselves financially through employment within a fifteen-month period. Ibid., 91.

Another study of a short-term prison-based reentry program providing participants with intensive transitional services in job readiness, substance abuse relapse prevention, basic living skills, homelessness prevention, and cognitive skills training found that the intervention participants performed significantly worse than did members of a comparison group on multiple measures of recidivism after one year. James A. Wilson and Robert C. Davis, "Good Intentions Meet Hard Realties: An Evaluation of the Project Greenlight Reentry Program," *Criminology & Public Policy* 5, no. 2 (May 2006): 303–38. For a response see Edward E. Rhine and others, "Implementation: The Bane of Effective Corrections Programs," *Criminology & Public Policy* 5, no. 2 (May 2006): 347–58.

60. U.S. Department of Justice, Federal Bureau of Prisons, Education Branch, Occupational Training Programs Directory, "Learning Skills for Work," September 2006. In 2000, all federal prisons offered some type of education programs with 93.5 percent of these prisons providing vocational training. Caroline Wolf Harlow, "Education and Correctional Populations," U.S. Department of Justice, Office of Justice Programs, Bureau of Justice Statistics, January 2003, revised April 15, 2003, NCJ 195670, 4 (Table 3 Educational

programs offered in State, Federal, and private prisons, 2000 and 1995, and local jails, 1999).

61. Diana Brazzell and others, *From the Classroom to the Community: Exploring the Role of Education during Incarceration and Reentry* (Washington, DC: Urban Institute, 2009), 12 (Table 3 Involvement in Correctional Education Programs by Type). In 1997, 45 percent of all federal inmates were involved in an education program since their admissions with 29 percent of all federal inmates receiving some type of vocational training. U.S. General Accounting Office, "Prison Release: Trends and Information on Reintegration Programs," June 2001, GAO-01-483, 16 (Table 5 Inmate Participation in Prison Programs in 1997). Other government sources indicated that 31 percent of all federal inmates received some vocational training in 1997. Harlow, "Education and Correctional Populations," 4 (Table 4 Participation in educational programs since most recent incarceration or sentence, for State and Federal prison inmates, 1997 and 1991, for local jail inmates 1996, and for probationers, 1995).

62. Federal Bureau of Prisons, "Education, Vocational & Job Training," http://www.bop.gov/inmate_programs/edu.jsp (accessed November 22, 2010) and UNICOR Federal Prison Industries, Inc., http://www.bop.gov/inmate_programs/unicor.jbp (accessed October 28, 2010).

63. U.S. Department of Justice, "Federal Bureau of Prisons, Program Statement, Inmate Work and Performance Pay," Program Statement 5251.06, October 1, 2008, Purpose and Scope §545.20a.

64. GAO, "Prison Release," 16 (Table 5 Inmate Participation in Prison Programs in 1997).

65. U.S. Department of Justice, Office of the Inspector General, Audit Division, Federal Prison Industries, Inc., "Annual Management Report," Fiscal Year 2010, December 2010, Audit Report 11-06, 3.

66. U.S. Department of Justice, Office of the Inspector General, Audit Division, "The Federal Bureau of Prisons Inmate Release Preparation and Transitional Reentry Programs," March 2004, Audit Report 04-16, iv, 28.

67. William G. Saylor and Gerald G. Gaes, "Training Inmates through Industrial Work Participation and Vocational and Apprenticeship Instruction," *Corrections Management Quarterly* 1, no. 2 (Spring 1997): 32–43, at 39–40, 42. See also William G. Saylor and Gerald G. Gaes, "PREP Study Links UNICOR Work Experience with Successful Post-Release Outcome," Federal Bureau of Prisons, Office of Research and Evaluation, revised January 8, 1992; William G. Saylor and Gerald G. Gaes, "The Differential Effect of Industries and Vocational Training on Postrelease Outcomes for Ethnic and Racial Groups: Research Note," *Corrections Management Quarterly* 5, no. 4 (Fall 2001): 17–24, at 23, concluded that minority groups benefited more from vocational training and industries participation than their nonminority counterparts. Cindy J. Smith and others, "Correctional Industries Preparing Inmates for Re-Entry: Recidivism & Post-Release Employment," Final Report, May 10, 2006, concluded that state prison inmates participating in Prison Industries Enhancement Certification Programs return to prison less frequently and entered postrelease employment more successfully than similar inmates participating in traditional prison industries or other-than-work activities while in prison.

Another study analyzed a sample of 1987 prison releasees from federal prisons found that participating in at least one-half (0.5) educational programs for each six months of prison time reduced the risk of rearrest or parole revocation within three years after release by about 39 percent. Miles D. Harer, "Prison Education Program and Recidivism: A Test of the Normalization Hypothesis," Federal Bureau of Prisons, Office of Research and Education, May 1995. See also Miles D. Harer, "Recidivism among Federal Prisoners Released in 1987," Federal Bureau of Prisons, Office of Research and Evaluation, August 4, 1994, 4, 23.

But see Kathleen E. Maguire and others, "Prison Labor and Recidivism," *Journal of Quantitative Criminology* 4, no. 1 (March 1988): 3–18, who found virtually identical recidivism rates among prison industry participants and nonparticipants, when differences between the two groups on other characteristics were controlled. However, Seiter and Kadela, "Prisoner Reentry," 373–74, concluded that a vocational education and work programs reduced recidivism.

68.   Steve Aos and others, "Evidence-Based Adult Corrections Programs: What Works and What Does Not," Washington State Institute for Public Policy, January 2006, 3 (Exhibit 1: Adult Corrections: What Works?), 6, 7. See also Steve Aos and others, "The Comparative Costs and Benefits of Programs to Reduce Crime," Washington State Institute for Public Policy, Version 4.0, May 2001, 8 (Table 1 Summary of Program Economics [All Monetary Values in 2000 Dollars]), 31–32; Polly Phipps, "Research Findings on Adult Corrections' Programs: A Review," Washington State Institute for Public Policy, January 1999, 66–79.

For a summary of in-prison educational programs see Anna Crayton and Suzanne Rebecca Neusteter, "The Current State of Correctional Education," Paper presented at the Reentry Roundtable on Education, John Jay College of Criminal Justice, February 2008.

69.   Aos and others, "Evidence-Based Adult Corrections Programs," 3, 6. Community-based employment training, job search and job assistance programs for adult offenders reduced recidivism by 4.8 percent. Ibid., 6. See generally, Gerald G. Gaes, "The Impact of Prison Education Programs on Post-Release Outcomes," Paper presented at the Reentry Roundtable on Education, John Jay College of Criminal Justice, February 18, 2008, 11, concluding that the marginal costs of prison education programs pale in comparison to criminal justice cost savings, including reductions in arrests, convictions, and recommitments. Other analyses concluding that a variety of in-prison programs reduce recidivism include D.A. Andrews and others, "Does Correctional Treatment Work? A Clinically Relevant and Psychologically Informed Meta-Analysis," *Criminology* 28, no. 3 (August 1990): 369–404; Francis T. Cullen and Paul Gendreu, "Assessing Correctional Rehabilitation: Policy, Practice, and Prospects," in *Criminal Justice 2000: Policies, Processes, and Decisions of the Criminal Justice System,* vol. 3, U.S. Department of Justice, Office of Justice Programs, July 2000, NCJ 183410. However, David B. Wilson and others, "A Meta-Analysis of Corrections-Based Education, Vocation, and Work Programs for Adult Offenders," *Journal of Research in Crime and Delinquency* 37, no. 4 (November 2000): 347–68, noted the weak methodological character of many of the thirty-three experimental

and quasi-experimental evaluations of education, vocation, and work programs. See also David B. Wilson and others, "A Quantitative Review and Description of Corrections-Based Education, Vocation, and Work Programs," *Corrections Management Quarterly* 3, no. 4 (Fall 1999): 8–18.

70. Donna Lee Breazzano, "The Federal Bureau of Prison Shifts to a Skills-Based Model," *Corrections Today* 71, no. 6 (December 2009): 50–53, at 57.

71. U.S. Government Accountability Office, "Federal Bureau of Prisons: BOP has Mechanisms in Place to Address Most Second Chance Act Requirements and is Working to Implement an Initiative Designed to Reduce Recidivism," Briefing for Subcommittees on Commerce, Justice, Science, and Related Agencies, Committees on Appropriations, United States Senate and House of Representatives, June 30, 2010, GA0-10-854R; BOP and transmittal letter, David C. Maurer, Director, Homeland Security and Justice, U.S. Government Accountability Office to Barbara Mikulski, Richard Shelby, Alan Mollohan, Frank R. Wolf, July 14, 2010.

72. U.S. Department of Labor, "About RexO," http://www.doleta.gov/RExO/aboutREx0.cfm (accessed November 3, 2010); Fernandes-Alcantara, "Vulnerable Youth," 28–31.

73. U.S. Department of Education, "Grants to States for Workplace and Community Transition Training for Incarcerated Individuals," http://www.ed.gov/programs/transitiontraining/funding.html (accessed April 16, 2011). The benefits of postsecondary education while incarcerated, a topic beyond the scope of this work, are summarized in Laura E. Gorgol and Brian A. Sponsler, "Unlocking Potential: Results of a National Survey of Postsecondary Education in State Prisons," Institute for Higher Education Policies, May 2011; Laura Winterfield and others, "The Effects of Post-Secondary Correctional Education: Final Report," Urban Institute, Justice Policy Center, May 2009; Correctional Association of New York, "Education from the Inside, Out: The Multiple Benefits of College Programs in Prison," January 2009. See also American Council on Education, "Higher Education Behind Bars: Postsecondary Prison Education Programs Make a Difference," Updated October 14, 2008; Jeanne Contardo and Michelle Tolbert, "Prison Postsecondary Education: Bridging Learning from Incarceration to the Community," Paper presented at the Reentry Roundtable on Education, John Jay College of Criminal Justice, February 2008; Kevin Helliker, "In Prison, College Courses Are Few," *Wall Street Journal*, May 4, 2011, A4.

74. Harry J. Holzer, "Workforce Development and the Disadvantaged: New Directions for 2009 and Beyond," Urban Institute, Perspectives on Low-Income Working Families, Brief 7, September 2008, 5.

75. U.S. Government Accountability Office, "Opportunities to Reduce Potential Duplication in Government Programs, Save Tax Dollars, and Enhance Revenue," March 2011, GAO-111-318SP, 140. See also Damian Paletta, "Billions in Bloat Uncovered in Beltway," *Wall Street Journal*, March 1, 2011, A1; Damian Paletta, "Both Sides Embrace Government-Waste Study," *Wall Street Journal*, March 2, 2011, A2. The U.S. Government Accountability Office provided further details of the duplication of workforce education and training programs across multiple federal agencies in its report, Multiple Employment and Training Programs: Providing Information on

Colocating Services and Consolidating Administrative Structures Could Promote Efficiencies, January 2011, GAO-11-92. See also an earlier report, U.S. General Accounting Office, "Multiple Employment and Training Programs: Funding and Performance Measures for Major Programs," April 2003, GAO-03-589.

Beyond duplication of programs, waste and fraud may exist in federal job training programs. Tom A. Coburn, "Help Wanted: How Federal Job Training Programs are Failing Workers," February 2011, 28, provided an example of waste in the summer jobs WIA youth program. For an example of fraud in the Job Corps see Ibid., 30–31.

The U.S. House of Representatives, "House Committee on the Budget, The Path to Prosperity: Restoring America's Promise: Fiscal Year 2012 Budget Resolution," April 2011, 43, proposed consolidating the duplicative job training programs into a single, more accountable career scholarships program.

76. Eberts and Erickcek, "Federal Role," 6.

77. See generally, e.g., "White House Task Force for Disadvantaged Youth," Final Report, October 2003, 8–10, 53–84. For new approach to assessing the benefits and costs of the assistance provided by the One-Stop Centers see Jacobson, "Strengthening," 14–17.

78. Jon Baron and Isabel V. Sawhill, "Federal Programs for Youth," Brookings Institution, May 1, 2010.

79. Office of Budget and Management, "Fiscal Year 2012 Budget of the U.S. Government," 28. See also David Leonhardt, "For Federal Programs, A Taste of Market Discipline," *New York Times*, February 9, 2011, B1; Jim McTague, "A Better Idea from the U.K.," *Barron's*, February 21, 2011, 29; Martha Ann Overland, "Government and Nonprofits Experiment with New Approach on Financing," *Chronicle of Philanthropy*, February 24, 2011, 10.

80. Shawn Bushway and Peter Reuter, "Labor Markets and Crime," in *Crime Public Policies for Crime Control*, ed. James Q. Wilson and Joan Petersilia (San Francisco, CA: ICS, 2002), 221. See also Shawn Bushway, "Reentry and Prison Work Programs, Employment Dimensions of Reentry, Understanding the Nexus between Prisoner Reentry and Work," Urban Institute Reentry Roundtable, Discussion Paper, May 19–20, 2003, 14–15.

81. U.S. Congress, Congressional Budget Office, "CBO's 2011 Long-Term Budget Outlook," June 2011; U.S. Congress, Congressional Budget Office, "The Budget and Economic Outlook: An Update," August 2010; U.S. General Accountability Office, "The Federal Government's Long-Term Fiscal Outlook," January 2011 Update, GAO-11-451SP. One credit rating agency downgraded the federal government's AAA credit rating. Damian Paleta, "U.S. Loses Triple-A Credit Rating," *Wall Street Journal*, August 6–7, 2011, A1; Binyamin Appelbaum and Eric Dash, "S.& P. Downgrades Debt of U.S. for the First Time," *New York Times*, August 6, 2011, A1. See also John Steel Gordon, "A Short Primer on the National Debt," *Wall Street Journal*, August 29, 2011, A17.

82. The National Commission on Fiscal Responsibility and Reform, "The Moment of Truth," December 2010, 10. See also, e.g., Damian Paletta and others, "Deficit Outlook Darkens," *Wall Street Journal*, January 27, 2011,

A1; Jackie Calmes, "In Revision, a 10-Year Deficit of $9 Trillion is Forecast," *New York Times*, August 26, 2009, A4; Jonathan Weisman and Deborah Solomon, "Decade of Debt: $9 Trillion," *Wall Street Journal*, August 26, 2009, A1.

83.   Pew Center on the States, "Beyond California: States in Fiscal Peril," November 2009; National Governors Association and National Association of State Budget Officers, "The Fiscal Survey of States: An Update of State Fiscal Conditions," Spring 2011; Christopher W. Hoene and Michael A. Pagano, "City Fiscal Conditions in 2010, National League of Cities, Research Brief on American's Cities," October 2010, Issue 2010-3; Pew Center on the States, "The Widening Gap: The Great Recession's Impact on State Pension and Retiree Health Care Costs," April 2011. See also, e.g., John Hood, "The States in Crisis," *National Affairs* 6 (Winter 2011): 49–69, at 50–64; Conor Dougherty, "State Tax Haul Jumps 10.8%," *Wall Street Journal*, October 27, 2011, A3; Michael Cooper, "Warning by States as Tax Revenues Fail to Rebound," *New York Times*, October 20, 2011, A13; Monica Davey, "Families Feel Sharp Edge of State Budget Cuts," *New York Times*, September 7, 2011, A1; Michael A. Fletcher, "Deal has States Bracing for Cuts in Federal Aid," *Washington Post*, August 3, 2011, A6; Kelly Nolan, "Fall in Property-Tax Revenue Squeezes Cities," *Wall Street Journal*, July 16–17, 2011, A3; Sara Murray, "Strapped States Curb Spending on Safety Net," *Wall Street Journal*, June 4–5, 2011, A4; Michael Cooper, "Improved Tax Collections Can't Keep Pace with States' Fiscal Needs, Survey Finds," *New York Times*, June 2, 2011, A13; Conor Dougherty, "States See Upticks in Revenue, Costs," *Wall Street Journal*, June 2, 2011, A4; Karen Hube, "Instead of Signs of Recovery, a Sucker Punch for State Budgets," *Washington Post*, May 29, 2011, G7; Michael Cooper, "States Collect More Taxes, but Troubles Remain," *New York Times*, May 25, 2011, A13; Conor Dougherty and Michael Corkery, "Local Governments Hit as Tax Revenue Falters," *Wall Street Journal*, May 21–22, 2011, A5; Michael Cooper, "For States, A Glimmer of Hope on Deficits," *New York Times*, May 18, 2011, A11; Michael Cooper and Mary Williams Walsh, "Public Pensions Once Off Limits," Face Budget Cuts," *New York Times*, April 26, 2011, A1; Jeanette Neumann and Michael Corkery, "State Pension Plans Lose Grounds," *Wall Street Journal*, April 26, 2011, A2; Michael A. Fletcher, "States Face a Shortfall of $1.26 Trillion in Funds to Pay Retiree Benefits," *Washington Post*, April 26, 2011, A13; Michael Cooper, "States Pass Budget Pain to Cities as Cutbacks in Services Cascade," *New York Times*, March 24, 2011, A1; Mary Williams Walsh, "The Burden of Pensions on States," *New York Times*, March 11, 2011, B1; Sam Dillon, "Tight Budgets Mean Squeeze in Classrooms," *New York Times*, March 7, 2011, A1; Jeanette Neuman, "Battered Public Pensions Do Better," *Wall Street Journal*, March 7, 2011, A4; Conor Dougherty and Amy Merrick, "Governors Chop Spending," *Wall Street Journal*, February 7, 2011, A1; David Wessel, "What Sent States' Fiscal Picture into a Tailspin?," *Wall Street Journal*, January 27, 2011, A5; Michael Cooper and Mary William Walsh, "Mounting Debts by States Stoke Fears of Crisis," *New York Times*, December 4, 2010, A1; Michael Cooper, "Fiscal Woes Deepening for Cities, Report Says," *New York Times*, October 7, 2010, A14; Jennifer Steinhauer, "New Year but No Relief for Strapped States," *New York Times*,

January 6, 2010, A15; Amy Merrick, "States Draw Up Plans for Year of Even Bigger Budget Cuts," *Wall Street Journal*, November 12, 2009, A7; Abby Goodnough, "States Turning to Last Resorts in Budget Crisis," *New York Times*, June 22, 2009, A1.

84.   Quoted in Krissah Thompson, "The Motor City Mayor's Engine for Change," *Washington Post*, February 8, 2011, A1, at A16.

85.   Annie Gowen, "Untick in Charity Seen as Sign of Better Times," *Washington Post*, June 20, 2011, A3; Stephanie Strom, "Charitable Giving Rose Last Year for First Time Since 2007," *New York Times*, June 20, 2011, B3. But see Holly Hall and Heather Joslyn, "Giving's Recovery Lacks Momentum," *Chronicle of Philanthropy*, June 30, 2011, 1.

3

Near-Term Strategies, Programs, and Policies: Nonprofit Approaches to Rehabilitate the Disconnected and the Formerly Incarcerated

For the foreseeable future, local nonprofit organizations will play an increasing role in all phases of workforce development, including providing training (both hard and soft skills), placement, and retention. Throughout the nation, these community-based programs not only teach needed skills but also seek to address the broader problems, such as dependency on drugs (or alcohol) or a dysfunctional family situation, that keep the jobless out of the workplace, even in the best of economic times.

This chapter examines nonprofit approaches to rehabilitate the disconnected and ex-offenders, providing empirical evidence, wherever possible. It offers examples of successful employment-oriented programs for both groups of individuals and one program meeting the transportation dilemma facing many inner city residents. It examines a pioneering program operating small businesses that provide employment for at-risk youth and those with criminal convictions as well as another program focusing on an entrepreneurial training. In the near-term, although nonprofit programs do not provide an instant panacea, social entrepreneurs throughout the nation could emulate these programs using the best practices and strategies set forth in this chapter. The chapter also surveys the organizational structures and financing alternatives for the small businesses established by nonprofit organizations, makes recommendations for revising public policies to promote entrepreneurship, and highlights some of the problems associated with scaling-up nonprofit organizations. The chapter concludes with an example of a collaboration among public agencies and nonprofit entities that are focused on workforce development. To better align the needs of both individuals and employers, this fledgling program seeks to pull together local public sector and nonprofit organizations with a rehabilitative workforce development mission into a systematic package, a difficult but not impossible endeavor.

Nonprofit Efforts at Rehabilitation

Many nonprofits approach workforce development by working with disconnected youths and adults as well as ex-offenders as part of larger, broader-based organizations. D.C. Central Kitchen's Culinary Job Training Program exemplifies this model. Some, such as Getting Out and Staying Out (GOSO), the Center for Employment Opportunities (CEO), and the Safer Foundation, offer stand-alone programs for inmates and ex-offenders.

D.C. Central Kitchen: A Nonprofit Approach to Employment–Oriented Workforce Development for a Broad Range of Participants

The D.C. Central Kitchen, Inc. (DCCK), a Washington, DC-based nonprofit organization founded in 1988, strives to address the root causes of hunger among the unemployed with its Culinary Job Training (CJT) Program.[1] DCCK's overarching mission centers on using "food as a tool to strengthen bodies, empower minds, and build communities."[2] Beyond the scope of this book, the DCCK operates a food recycling and meal distribution program, both reclaiming unused food from restaurants and caterers and purchasing discounted "defective" produce from local farms, bringing the food and produce to a central location, where they are transformed into nourishing meals, then delivered to local nonprofit social service agencies. It also provides breakfast, outreach, and counseling services to chronically homeless individuals through its First Helping Program. Another program, Healthy Returns, brings healthy meals and snacks to agencies serving low-income children and at-risk youth throughout the region.[3] Given the focus of this work, DCCK seeks to train the "unemployable" for culinary careers.

Serving a rehabilitative function, the DCCK's CJT Program prepares the unemployed, the underemployed, previously incarcerated persons, and homeless adults for careers in the food service industry.[4] Employers get qualified, drug-free employees, and those in need of a good job obtain skills qualifying them for work in their field of interest.

The sixteen-week culinary curriculum, with all-day classes, Monday through Friday, covers all facets of work in a professional kitchen. The sixteen-week program is more demanding, more instructive than a one- or two-day seminar, but not as rigorous as a one- or two-year cooking school certificate. The program uses a hands-on approach rather than one centered around an academic, book-based classroom. Its culinary coordinator and local chefs, who volunteer once a week to teach specific skills, including cooking techniques and methods, cutting, various ingredients (fruits, vegetables, fresh herbs, grains, and pastas), stocks and sauces as well as meat, fish, and seafood cookery, offer demonstrations and answer industry-related questions. Students participate in a scheduled rotation at each production station throughout DCCK's commercial kitchen. Each station produces meals for delivery to the homeless, low-income individuals, and after-school programs. There they are trained and mentored by the station chefs and gain experience in various food stations. Students complete the ServSafe Food Protection Manager's Certification course, a nationally recognized food safety curriculum prepared by the National Restaurant Association's Educational Foundation. They also participate in a capstone one-week internship at a local hotel, restaurant, catering, or food service operation, where they work with mentoring chefs in a commercial kitchen to gain practical experience. During the program, the trainees receive a weekly stipend to cover the costs of transportation and the purchase of incidentals. At the end of the sixteen weeks, each graduate receives a diploma, for many the first diploma they ever have received.

The last four weeks of the program consist of a full-time job search. After career exploration classes where students initially examine their career goals, interests, and skills and then learn to fill out applications, write resumes, and interview successfully, they talk to job search counselors every morning and spend each day completing applications and going on interviews. They continue their search for full-time employment at local hospitality businesses.

Going beyond technical kitchen skills, the comprehensive program offers both soft skills training and self-empowerment services.

The program's Workforce Development Coordinator teaches the importance of job-readiness skills, including punctuality, resume writing, computer literacy, interviewing techniques, a positive work attitude, and teamwork.

Self-empowerment sessions provide a holistic approach to further each student's personal growth. These sessions focus on the thinking and behavioral modifications designed to move students from dependence to independence as well as to identify and reinforce personal life changes needed for success, including discussing triggers, coping strategies, and conflict resolution techniques. Values, such as accountability, time management, and financial responsibility, are developed.

Most of the students in the program are typically ex-offenders, sixty-eight out of ninety-one in a recent class.[5] A Transition Group for those released from incarceration within twelve months of enrollment in the program focuses on identifying and addressing the challenges associated with reentering society. Participants begin to learn strategies to cope with their negative emotions, among other self-defeating factors.

The CJT Program has achieved a great measure of success based, in part, on the strong connections it has built with local employers in the hospitality industry. In 2009, even in the midst of the Great Recession, eighty-one students graduated from the program, with an 80 percent job placement rate on graduation (down from the program's more typical 94 percent rate) at an average starting wage of $11.05 per hour and 73 percent job retention rate after six months of employment at an $11.54 per hour average wage. Ninety-five percent of these graduates passed the ServSafe exam and became certified food handlers.[6]

The DCCK also employs its graduates in its for-profit full-service company, Fresh Start Catering,[7] that provides catering for offices and school dining services, using local, seasonal, and sustainable ingredients whenever possible. There, the CJT Program graduates learn advanced skills and techniques to further prepare them for permanent employment in the food service industry, while generating revenues and lessening DCCK's reliance on grants and donations.

In contrast to a national average recidivism rate of 67 percent within three years, the graduates of the CJT Program generally evidence a recidivism rate of less than 2.5 percent.[8] Part of the success turns on the time and energy devoted to admitting students into the program. The application process is rigorous with twenty-five students

selected out of each group of seventy-five to one hundred applicants. The program utilizes a score card approach, including questions related to unresolved life pressures and chronic problems, such as substance abuse, to predict success. There is, however, a dropout rate of between 15 percent and 40 percent for each entering class.[9] Even some of the dropouts show up several months later "cleaned up" and ready to reenter the program with a new sense of determination.

Getting Out and Staying Out: Facilitating Offender Reentry

One of the most successful nonprofit reentry programs, Getting Out and Staying Out, Inc. (GOSO), founded in 2003, offers a series of coordinated services, before and after release designed to facilitate economic independence through purposeful education and directed employment.[10] The program does not, however, use transitional jobs as a reentry technique.

By getting in and staying involved with inmates, GOSO has lowered the recidivism rate of the young men incarcerated in Rikers Island, New York City's largest jail. As reported by the organization, less than 20 percent of GOSO's clients return to jail or prison, compared with an overall Rikers recidivism rate of roughly 66 percent.[11] Working with young prisoners, who have not been in jail for a long period, increases the odds of success. However, even this select group faces steep hurdles after release.

GOSO's program brings volunteers, generally retired, successful business executives, to the jail to work with eighteen- to twenty-four-year-old prisoners on a weekly basis, even before they finish their sentences. The volunteers provide the inmates with practical direction and the tools to build productive lives in mainstream society, through education and job training. GOSO's staff then continue to provide transitional services to coach the ex-offenders when they return to their respective communities throughout New York City, with mentoring provided by volunteers.

GOSO works with young prisoners to plan for reentry from the day they are accepted into the program after submitting an essay and a resume and signing a contract, typically the day of their incarceration or shortly thereafter. It strives to stick with them over the long term.

The program begins inside Horizon Academy, a joint program of the New York City Education and Correction Departments, the voluntary school at the Rikers Island facility, where GOSO participants study for their high school diploma or General Educational Development (GED) certificate. In addition, they receive one-to-one and group mentoring on successful living and soft skills fundamentals, such as showing up daily and working hard, access to role models, and psychosocial counseling. The volunteers, as former business executives, know who gets hired and promoted in various industries. They impart to the inmates how to turn an entry-level position the ex-offenders will initially obtain into a viable career. In sum, GOSO brings a business perspective, rather than a social service viewpoint, into the program, emphasizing motivational principles, including perseverance and ambition, designed to help build a career.

When the inmates cycle out of Rikers Island and are incarcerated in upstate New York prisons, GOSO writes to them regularly, checks on their progress, and sends them books and study materials to continue to fuel their development and prepare them for their successful transition back into the community. GOSO strives to keep each inmate-participant focused on the future and ensure that he takes advantage of any programs that exist in the incarceration facility.

On release from Rikers Island or a prison, about 50–60 percent of those come to GOSO's storefront office. On a first visit, GOSO has helped the organization determine his immediate housing, counseling, and treatment needs. Referrals are made to agencies that provide various services, such as substance abuse, mental health, and emergency housing needed to establish stability in one's life. He leaves the office with the essential reentry tools needed to be on time, to be prepared, and to be safe. These include an alarm clock, a note pad, pens, a weekly planner, condoms, a metro fare card, and a resume. Each also leaves with a plan for the immediate future that will guide him through his search for an entry-level position or an education that will lead to meaningful employment. Thereafter, they check in once a week for the first three months, as they develop and implement their reentry plans. The one-to-one and group mentoring and coaching continues at GOSO's office, along with workshops, seminars, and counseling.

GOSO clients have access to GOSO's career counselors, who work in the community to establish relationships with employers that will hire its clients in positions offering adequate pay, reasonable benefits, and opportunities for advancement into a rewarding career. The career counselors discuss with clients current employment possibilities, recommend organizations that offer training programs and apprenticeships, and employers offering flexibility to accommodate a client's engagement in education. GOSO also works with a local job finder to discover employment leads. With its partner organizations in the areas of social services, health care, education, vocational training, and legal advocacy, GOSO strives to meet the special needs of each participant.

In addition to reducing recidivism, GOSO's program increases the prospects for employment or further education on release. About three-quarters of the former prisoners are employed or attend school, according to the organization.[12]

Center for Employment Opportunities: A Transitional Jobs Reentry Model

While GOSO works with participants while they are incarcerated and thereafter, the Center for Employment Opportunities, Inc. (CEO) provides comprehensive employment services to released individuals with recent criminal convictions.[13] CEO, a nonprofit organization founded in 1996, based in New York City, with offices in Albany, Buffalo, Rochester, and Syracuse, with recently launched sites in Oakland and San Diego, California and Tulsa, Oklahoma, helps some 3,400 ex-offenders annually prepare for, locate, and retain jobs through its paid short-term transitional employment program, while also providing job development assistance using its employment reentry model. It works with releasees, parolees, and probationers. Typically, more than 90 percent (94 percent) of CEO participants are males, one-third are between ages eighteen and twenty-five, 70 percent are fathers, and about 60 percent (59 percent) are black.[14]

Through CEO's Neighborhood Work Project,[15] the organization provides immediate transitional employment and, thus, valuable work experience and a reference. After finishing a four-day preemployment life skills class, each participant receives time-limited employment at a minimum wage job for some two to three months, with CEO trying to move clients to permanent positions as soon as they are able. The day labor assignments, four days a week, provide structure in participants' lives and help develop good work habits, such as punctuality and teamwork, thereby making clients more employable and helping them retain permanent positions. Paying participants daily gives them immediate spending money, while reinforcing their dependability. Each of work crews has a full-time field supervisor who teaches the use of tools and equipment required for the job as well as basic soft skills, including taking directions and working hard. Transitional work offers the chance to teach these soft skills on the job, through coaching and trial-and-error, before placement in a permanent position. The supervisors evaluate participants daily on a scale of 1 to 5 on CEO's Company Principles of Success: cooperation with supervisor, effort at work, on time, cooperation with co-workers, and personal presentation. During the transitional jobs phase, participants can be terminated for refusing to work or verbally abusing a supervisor or a co-worker. They are also subject to disciplinary measures for tardiness or absenteeism, among other infractions.

CEO's transitional work component is mainly self-funded. The work crews perform tasks on contract basis, with about 80 percent, on average, of the program's costs, i.e., salaries and benefits to work crews and supervisors, covered by payments for the work performed. CEO has contracts with public sector agencies to provide building maintenance, janitorial, groundskeeping, and painting, among other services. In contrast to CEO's transitional work component, the costs of the job development, placement, and retention services are supported by donations and public sector grants.

Along with the transitional work experience, CEO offers participants permanent job placement assistance through its Vocational Development Program, preplacement training, and postplacement services. Participants initially receive one-on-one counseling from CEO job coaches designed to identify and address future workplace problems, so that they are ready for regular employment. The preplacement training for participants in New York City offers short programs that teach entry-level skills, including customer service, warehouse/forklift, construction industry tasks, and sanitation. Life skills classes address behavioral and skills gaps related to finding and keeping a job and how to answer potential employers' questions related to criminal history. Once job ready, they develop an employment plan and receive job placement assistance from CEO's staff that matches work histories, skills, training, and occupational interests with employers' needs from entry-level employees. Participants meet with CEO job developers once a week to seek a permanent job while continuing to maintain their transitional job/work crew position and working with their job coaches.

CEO also offers ongoing services for individuals placed in jobs, typically in customer service, food industries, warehouse, and office support, for one year to help them stay in their positions and begin to move up the career ladders. To ensure employer satisfaction, CEO staff regularly check with firms by telephone to monitor progress and mediate any issues, when necessary.

After each month of retaining their jobs, participants are eligible for the organization's Rapid Rewards Program that provides noncash incentives, such as grocery store vouchers and public transportation fare cards, to those who meet employment retention milestones designed to keep them connected to the labor force and to the organization's support services. The incentives not only encourage participants to provide employment documentation CEO needs for its funders, but also help improve job retention by encouraging them to remain in contact with the organization's staff or increase the financial pay off from continued employment.[16]

According to one study, participants enrolled in the Rapid Rewards Program were more likely to make the 90-, 180-, and 365-day milestones and used more CEO services compared to a control group who did not enroll in the program.[17] The Rapid Rewards Program appeared to make the greatest difference for participants with the lowest starting wages. Participants considered at a higher risk of job loss postplacement also receive intensive support services, including frequent visits to the workplace by CEO staff, and continued counseling and career planning. Less intensive services include monthly staff visits at worksites.

For all participants, CEO's comprehensive program also include various support services and the CEO Academy. CEO provides assistance and referrals in helping deal with other issues ex-offenders face, including housing and medical care. Its Responsible Fatherhood Program advises noncustodial fathers how to pay child support at a level they can afford. Its parenting programs offer participants in the Responsible Fatherhood Program the opportunity to strengthen their relationships with their children through parenting classes and workshops, including proper discipline and children's developmental stages. The pioneering CEO Academy, a partnership between the organization and the community colleges in the City University of New York system (CUNY), helps participants progress from entry-level jobs into the skilled trades. In the eight-month program, CEO provides academic preparation to participants to help them enroll in and complete skilled trades courses at CUNY community colleges.

CEO has achieved success both with respect to employment and recidivism. According to internal management information system statistics, from 1992 to 1996, CEO placed 70 percent of its participants in permanent, full-time employment, typically within two or three months after entering the program.[18] Those not placed failed to show up for job development services or were terminated for not following work crew rules. The average wage for placements in 1996, a period of relatively full employment, for example, was almost 50 percent above minimum wage, with two-thirds of the jobs offering benefits. In 1996, the job retention was 75 percent after one month, 60 percent after three months, and 38 percent after six months. However, only about one quarter (26 percent) of all participants were on the road to success as measured by holding a job for a substantial time period. Subsequently, in the twelve-month period from July 1, 2008 through June 30, 2009, the six-month job retention rates for participants equaled 55 percent, a 22 percent increase compared to the previous twelve-month period.[19]

An initial evaluation of CEO's Young Adult Program suggests its approach is also successful. This program provides specialized social services that are more personalized and supportive in a nurturing environment for at-risk young ex-offenders adults, ages eighteen to twenty-five, who have little or no employment history or educational background and/or who face high barriers to regular, full-time employment, such as a lack of family and peer support. Program participants were significantly more likely to remain at CEO past nine days of transitional work, an early attrition benchmark, than a control group of young adults who did not participate in the program, 70 percent versus 59 percent. The intervention group was 1.4 times more likely to be placed in a job than the control group.[20] Ex-offenders also benefit from the general CEO Prisoner Reentry Program.

Recent independent evaluations found that the CEO Prisoner Reentry Program had no statistical impact on employment, earnings, or job characteristics after one year,[21] but it lowered recidivism through two years of follow up.[22] After two years, the program group had an arrest rate of 37.7 percent, compared to 41.8 percent for the control group, whose members only received basic job search assistance. The intervention group had a conviction rate of 30.5 percent after two years, compared to 38.3 percent for the control group. The program group was less likely to be convicted of a violent crime, 4.4 percent versus 5.8 percent for the control group. After two years, the intervention group was less likely to be reincarcerated 49.5 percent versus 55.4 percent for the control group, with only 13.9 percent of the program

group reincarcerated for a new crime compared to 16.9 percent for the control group. For those in the high risk of reoffending subgroup, the program significantly reduced the probability of rearrest, the probability of reconviction, and the number of rearrests by the end of the second, but not the first, follow-up year. There were few, if any, program impacts on recidivism for former prisoners in the low and medium risk of reoffending subgroups.[23] In sum, high-risk offenders benefited most from CEO's transitional jobs program, at least after two years.

After three years, for those coming to the program as recent releasees (the program group), the program group had an arrest rate of 49.1 percent, compared to 59.1 percent for the control group. The intervention group had a conviction rate of 44 percent, compared to 56.7 percent for the control group, a 22 percent difference. The program group was far less likely to be convicted of a violent crime, 5.4 percent versus 14.3 percent for the control group. After three years, the intervention group was less likely to be reincarcerated 60.2 percent versus 71.3 percent for the control group, with 25.1 percent of the program group reincarcerated for a new crime compared to 34.1 percent for the control group, a more than 26 percent difference.[24]

In contrast to the CEO program, another study found, however, that transitional jobs programs in four Midwestern cities, Chicago, Detroit, Milwaukee, and St. Paul, had little or no impact on employment and recidivism.[25] Researchers randomly assigned more than 1,800 male ex-offenders to either a transitional jobs (jt) program or to a program providing basic job search (js) assistance but no temporary jobs. The first-year results found that the jt group was no more likely to work in an unsubsidized job in the formal labor market than the js group and overall, except that the transitional jobs program may have been more effective in weaker labor markets. The jt programs had no consistent impacts on recidivism during the first-year follow-up, with about one-third of each group rearrested and returned to prison, but the men in the jt group were less likely to be reincarcerated for a parole violation.

Safer Foundation: Another Employment Reentry Model

The Safer Foundation, a Chicago-based nonprofit organization founded in 1972,[26] offers pre and postrelease employment and education services, but its efforts do not focus on transitional jobs, with the exception of one pilot program that placed clients in ninety days of full-time employment with one major private employer.[27] Also, in contrast to CEO, Safer operates two residential work release facilities in Chicago on behalf of the Illinois Department of Corrections. These centers give individuals who are nearing release from Illinois supervision the support and services needed to reestablish ties to family, employment, and community.[28]

At the heart of Safer's postrelease services, clients begin a six-hour group orientation and intake session, which includes screening for potential barriers to employment, such as substance abuse, and referral to Safer's Supportive Services Department for various assessments and counseling. Then clients go on to its Retention Services where each meets with an employment case manager. These meetings assist clients confront the task of obtaining and maintaining employment on reentry. Clients must attend a week-long job-readiness training program, which includes instructions in filling out applications, developing a resume, and preparing for an interview. Then they participate in retention group sessions, overseen by a Safer retention specialist, where clients hunt for job leads and vent their frustrations and fears about the process. Once a client finds a job, the retention specialist follows up weekly for the first thirty days, gauges the status of the transition, and offers support, if needed. If a placement does not work out, the organization provides a replacement worker, thereby reducing the adverse impact on the hiring company. Safer's employment services section, Pivotal Staffing, LLC, places clients in the workforce and provides employers with recruitment assistance and logistical services. The firms are in various fields, including transportation, distribution, hospitality, landscaping, and manufacturing.

Safer's workforce programs serve nearly 13,000 clients each year, with about 3,800 clients placed in employment. According to one independent study, Illinois state prison releasees recidivate at a 51.8 percent rate after three years. Safer's clients who achieve thirty days of employment recidivate at a 22 percent rate, a 58 percent reduction. Clients employed for twelve consecutive months recidivate at an 8 percent rate.[29] In sum, Safer's postrelease programs provide training and job placement services typically without transitional jobs. Its program is, therefore, less expensive than CEO's but a comparison of the cost-effectiveness of these two models does not exist.

To round out Safer's offerings, its Youth Empowerment Program offers an intensive eight-week GED program for at-risk youth, ages sixteen to twenty-one, who have criminal records and have not completed high school.[30] This small group, peer-based educational skills program, under the guidance of trained facilitators, offers GED examination preparation. In 2011, the program achieved an 81 percent passage rate for the GED exam.[31]

Strategies for Nonprofit Employment-Oriented Workforce Development Programs

This section analyzes the various aspects of building a successful employment-oriented workforce development program that nonprofit organizations must focus on, including demand-driven training, job placement and retention, a comprehensive approach, support provided by mentors, accountability, mission clarity, and financial stability. Furthermore, the special problems faced by employment reentry programs for ex-offenders are also discussed, as well as the additional steps these programs must take, for example, developing a network of employers willing to hire individuals with a criminal record, in order to be successful.

A Demand-Approach to Workforce Development

Nonprofit organizations must center their workforce development efforts on demand-driven skills training that serve the needs of both individuals and businesses. Rather than looking merely to get someone any job, as do the core services offered by One-Stop Centers, discussed in Chapter 3, nonprofit organizations must train for jobs in growing fields, such as health care and medical devices, with advancement opportunities, locally, regionally, and statewide. Granted, forecasting where jobs will be on completion of training, never mind years in the future, is difficult. The effort must, however, be made to assess unmet labor demands, and then integrate skills training and work readiness with individualized case management services as needed.

Nonprofit organizations must track which jobs are most in demand, at least in the near-term, and direct their programs accordingly. Avoiding both outdated career paths and not using equipment and techniques that are no longer relevant, they must gear programs to local and regional job markets and labor market trends.

In implementing demand-driven training, nonprofit entities must strive to treat employers as clients. They develop and win firms' trust by meeting commercial needs. Providing workers with skills and behaviors employers seek rests on developing close links to local employers, so that training better meets labor market demands.

Nonprofit organizations must work and partner with local employers to identify their needs, particularly in-demand jobs that provide both entry-level opportunities and future career ladders for less-skilled workers. An experimental research design study, using an intervention group and a control group, of three sectoral-focused workforce development programs showed five positive outcomes in terms of total earnings, likelihood of employment, hours worked, hourly wages, and availability of benefits.[32] The nonprofit organizations in this study focused on an industry or a small set of industries and developed both industry-specific expertise and relationships with employers that supported the training programs' design, implementation, and ongoing adaptation. In short, training ought to flow from a dual focus designed to meet the needs of both employers and unskilled individuals.

As with the disconnected youths and adults, there exists a mismatch between the massive, annual influx of ex-offenders and available jobs. Additionally, job training and employment programs must review the federal and state laws and regulations that limit the employment of those with criminal convictions, particularly ex-felons, as noted in Chapter 2. These exclusionary laws often cover all felony convictions, including any offenses unrelated to the occupation in question, and generally do not account for the years that may have intervened following an offense.

Job Placement and Retention

Job placement and retention cannot be overlooked. With proper identification of in-demand jobs, skills training generally does not constitute the problem; rather it is placement, especially in a recession. To surmount job placement difficulties, nonprofit organizations need to develop strong relationships with local employers. Intermediaries that provide weak applicants are viewed as social service agencies, not service providers responsive to employer needs.

Effective nonprofit–for-profit partnerships constitute a two-way street. In addition to supplying businesses needing qualified, work-ready applicants, nonprofit organizations help employers in a variety of ways. They serve as staffing agents for small- and medium-size firms lacking a human resources department. After discussing and assessing an employer's personnel needs, they can evaluate a possible fit between an employer and job seekers' interests and skills. They can screen individuals carefully for job readiness and skills, send only qualified applicants for interviews, vouch that those they refer will be capable workers, and provide addition supervision, if needed, to ensure that any new hire follows through. By offering information upfront about applicants, they can save employers the cost of conducting background checks on prospective employees. Using an intermediary that performs quality screening and refers only qualified applicants will significantly reduce any employers' liability risks resulting from the alleged negligent hiring of ex-offenders. In sum, local community-based groups can offer support services by matching qualified ex-offender applicants with available positions, and providing training, prescreening, and ongoing services to employers, thereby helping employers absorb some of the risks and costs of hiring ex-offenders.

In the placement process, reentry programs must focus on employers and industries, more generally, not adverse to hiring ex-inmates. Industries most willing to hire people with criminal convictions are those requiring little customer contact, such as manufacturing, construction, transportation, and behind-the-scene food service. Retail and service industries are those most unwilling to hire ex-offenders.[33] Even in the absence of legal barriers, placement is less likely in the retail and service fields, especially where tasks require contact with customers, handling cash, or expensive merchandise.

To meet the critical challenge of job placement for ex-inmates, especially ex-felons, nonprofit organizations must develop a network of employers willing to hire ex-offenders with minimal skills (or no work experience). Building relationships with employers and maintaining their trust and confidence is key to the placement of ex-offenders.

Following a successful job placement, nonprofit organizations often neglect job retention, a critical task. It is difficult to keep the disconnected and ex-offenders in jobs, even if placed. The first six months or so on the job is often critical. Although expensive and time consuming, ongoing support to help ensure success ought to be provided.

Postplacement job retention and support services include referrals for child care[34] and transportation[35] assistance that if left unattended often interfere with job success. Nonprofit organizations can also help resolve any problems that may arise between an employee and an employer by taking the initiative and addressing issues that might compromise the work relationship. An intermediary ideally would need a staff person (or persons) to work with those placed in jobs and employers to help keep program participants employed. Weekly contacts with employers are initially helpful, along with meetings with immediate job supervisors to discuss job performance issues, including punctuality, attention to detail, and ability to get along with co-workers. Building this type of postplacement relationship takes money and time. Intermediaries must also be mindful that working through a third party may be burdensome for employers dealing with their employees.

A Comprehensive Approach

The success of the DCCK's CJT Program is based, in part, on the promise that achieving sustained, permanent employment requires an integrated, holistic approach, not merely job and soft skills training. This comprehensive strategy is expensive and time consuming. In addition to providing general employment and specific job skills, the CJT Program offers intensive life skills training to address many of the obstacles, such as a lack of self-confidence, that previously impeded participants from becoming and remaining employed. It offers exposure to and training in the social skills the workplace requires and job placement counseling. Participants learn the socialization of work norms, including strictly enforced behavioral rules, such as the need to get up every morning, show up on time, stick with a task and not get discouraged easily, follow directions, accept a subordinate relationship and not react negatively when told what to do, and effective communication skills. The program also emphasizes character development: discipline, hard work, perseverance, motivation, self-control, sociability, emotional stability, and anger management.

The comprehensive approach also addresses prevalent mental health needs and the current impact of past family abuse and violence. Because few organizations possess the in-house capacity to meet all these needs, nonprofit organizations need to refer participants to other entities equipped to address these issues. In addition to breaking self-destructive behaviors, such as substance abuse, successful programs strive to change attitudes, particularly a negative mentality marked by self-doubt and a resignation to unemployment, that lead to replicating poverty cycles. In short, these programs strive to inspire a belief in one's nearly limitless potential.

As shown by GOSO, CEO, and Safer, successful reentry programs also use broader, comprehensive systems. They help with the foundational problems in ex-offenders' lives, such as obtaining housing and substance abuse treatment. They assist with the collection of documents needed for employment, for example, Social Security cards, and provide legal assistance in dealing with outstanding arrest warrants and child support arrearages. Comprehensive reentry programs foster collaborations with the community and enhance informal social control mechanisms. Support for the formerly incarcerated rests on effective partnerships among service providers, law enforcement officers, family members, and the community-at-large.

Support Provided by Mentors

Disconnected youths and adults as well as ex-offenders often need one-to-one mentors throughout the rehabilitative process. Mentoring connects a vulnerable youth with a responsible individual who can assist in navigating safe pathways to adulthood.[36] Today's inner city youth, who often lack ties to their fathers and other males in mainstream society (as discussed in Chapter 1), face many social and psychological demands, including negative peer pressures, substance abuse, past child and family violence, depression as well as poor nutrition and health care practices. While focusing on the potential failures of young adults, such as avoiding crime, drugs, and nonmarital pregnancies, by providing sound role models and guidance, mentors offer lasting, positive ties, based on confidence, trust, and respect. They provide sustenance of the most personal kind. An ongoing relationship with a caring adult represents a key component to healthy development of each of these at-risk youths.

Mentoring, a supportive one-on-one relationship, also assists to integrate ex-prisoners into society and deal with the initial transition months.[37] Mentors help address multiple interrelated reentry needs, including employment, physical and mental health, substance abuse prevention and treatment, stable housing, and family reconnection. They provide assistance in the postplacement, job retention phase, for three to six months.

In helping others make the transition to postincarceration society, successful ex-offenders generally make the best mentors. Programs also ought to consider seniors as a source of mentors. Rather than volunteer mentors, a need exists for trained, full-time, and paid mentors, who are available 24/7. These full-time, always available mentors could help the formerly incarcerated with interpersonal difficulties, such as a pregnant girlfriend, a sick mother, or a brother in trouble with the law, and life's challenges, including the loss of a job or substance abuse problems. Mentors assist in fostering self-confidence, promoting a sense of responsibility, and dealing with negative family and neighborhood influences. For ex-inmates who become easily discouraged at work or get mad when a supervisor tells them what to do, a mentor can help deal with these problems and prevent the rapid fall into the category of chronically unemployed persons, who return to a life of crime. In sum, mentors assist releasees with prosocial integration activities, attitudes, and behaviors.

The best mentoring relationships for the disconnected and ex-offenders provide a structured support program.[38] These structured efforts create a relationship of trust between mentor and mentee, an established contact pattern, parameters for meetings and activities, and a timeframe commitment. In addition to a plan for the recruitment, screening, and orientation of potential mentors and a strategy to match mentors and mentees, a mentoring program requires ongoing training and supervision for mentors, coupled with consistent evaluation and assessment. The administrators and staff responsible for programmatic implementation also require training and technical assistance.

Accountability, Mission-Focused, Financially Responsible

As with the public sector agencies analyzed in Chapter 2, nonprofit organizations must implement accountability measures. Focusing on performance data and measurable results, each needs to identify and quantify the outcomes its program seeks to achieve. Evaluation findings must be translated into guidance for nonprofit leaders and staff. Efficiency and productivity, getting the maximum results from the minimum amount of resources, must serve as watchwords. Public sector agencies must be accountable not only for their own efforts but also for the nonprofit organizations they fund.

Nonprofit organizations must achieve a clarity of mission, focusing on and sticking to what they do best. While being flexible and adapting their mission to serve the cause of workforce development and their clients, nonprofit organizations must avoid losing their focused mission.

Funding for small tax-exempt organizations is often precarious, reliant on a few key donors. Providing secure, adequate funding is essential. Nonprofit organizations ought to maintain diversified funding sources, including foundations, individuals, corporations, and the public sector, so they do not need to cater to any one entity or group. If one funding source (or a group of steady donors) drops off or out, the entity will not fold.[39]

It is important to note that in connecting outcomes, mission, and funding, nonprofit organizations face a key problem. Although often

initiated and run by charismatic, tenacious, committed founders and leaders, who operate pragmatically, these dedicated individuals are subject to burnout, thereby placing the organization's survival in jeopardy. Nonprofit organizations must train and mentor successor leadership.

Overcoming the Lack of Transportation to Jobs

A lack of transportation prevents many individuals from accessing (and retaining) jobs located away from inner cities. Public mass transit systems bring commuters into the city. They generally do not take lower skilled, less educated inner city residents to higher growth businesses and jobs in the suburbs. Those who are poor usually cannot afford reliable transportation. Bus transportation is often not useful, particularly for inner city residents who locate a job in the suburbs and/or who do not work during the traditional 9:00 a.m. to 5:00 p.m. hours. Those who can afford to buy a car, often purchase vehicle from a "buy here pay here" used car lot. These sellers charge high interest rates because the purchasers do not qualify for traditional, lower interest rate auto loans. These used cars typically have high mileage that often equals frequent and expensive repairs and lower gas mileage.

One study highlighted the barrier transportation presented to employability. More than one-third of both intervention group (the Opportunity to Succeed Program designed to reduce substance abuse relapse and recidivism by providing comprehensive reentry services to ex-felons with drug offense histories) and the control group, 39.1 percent and 32.9 percent, respectively, reported difficulties in obtaining a car for work or emergencies. Some 27 percent (27.3 percent) of the program group and about 17 percent (17.5 percent) of the control group encountered difficulties using public transportation, with about 17 percent of both groups, 16.6 percent of the intervention group and 17.5 percent of the control group, having faced making costly car repairs.[40]

To attempt to deal with these catch-22 transportation dilemmas, car ownership programs, pioneered by nonprofit organizations,[41] help low-income residents buy used cars for dependable transportation to and from work, thereby overcoming the spatial mismatch that separates inner city residents from the centers of job growth in suburban areas. These car programs also help recipients take their children to school and get to supermarkets and pharmacies often located outside their neighborhoods.

One program, Wheels of Success, Inc. (WoS), a Tampa, Florida-based nonprofit organization, assists financially strapped, working individuals find affordable, reliable transportation so they can retain their employment and sustain their independence.[42] Founded in 2003, the program takes cars purchased or donated by individuals and dealerships, fixes them up through the support of its partners in the automotive industry, and "sells" them to low-income recipients. From its founding through June 30, 2011, it provided 456 vehicles to recipients. Using a "pay it forward" approach, WoS requires its vehicle recipients to "buy" used cars with monthly charges based on their ability to pay, typically about $50 a month for one year. Repayments help the organization continue its mission by funding car acquisitions and repairs for others in need. Program recipients must be employed full-time and in need of transportation to continue working and supporting themselves and their families (or unable to return to work because of transportation issues). They must be nominated by a local social service agency, a religious organization, or an employer, be "working poor," with income of up to 250 percent above the poverty level, and ineligible for public sector-provided assistance, except for unemployment compensation, Medicaid, food stamps, and subsidized housing. Their financial situation must leave them unable to buy a vehicle. If accepted into the program, they must donate three service hours per month for twelve months to the organization.

Nonprofit Organizations Form and Operate Small Businesses as a Workforce Development Strategy

To enable those at risk as well as ex-offenders gain hands-on job training and other skills and provide temporary employment, nonprofit organizations can organize and operate one or more small businesses. These entities may even provide long-term employment for participants. Profits from the revenue-generating businesses may partially fund a nonprofit organization's social mission.

Homeboy Industries (HI), a nonprofit organization based in Los Angeles, pioneered in creating series of small businesses to teach young adults hands-on employment skills, both hard and soft.[43] The organization's gang intervention program, the nation's largest, developed more than two decades ago by its founder, Father Gregory Boyle, infuses hope in those whom hope is foreign, using jobs to draw youths away from gangs.

Gangs arise for many reasons: pride, territoriality, and security.[44] Individuals often turn to gangs when no viable family support structure exists. Also, jails and prisons are dangerous places. New inmates join gangs for protection and connections. Gang loyalties are then exported back to neighborhoods. The reoccurring pattern of recidivism strengthens gang ties, with many gangs representing criminal organizations that terrorize and impoverish communities. They may control a neighborhood's streets. By impeding the ability of ex-inmates to reintegrate successfully into the community, continued gang membership limits the possibilities for engaging in prosocial bonds and provides additional opportunities that reinforce negative peer interactions.

Becoming an independent nonprofit organization in August 2001, HI has helped thousands of young adults, ages fourteen to thirty, considered at risk, particularly those recently released from incarceration, find work. About 85 percent of the 12,000 current and former gang members from hundreds of Los Angeles gangs who turn to HI each year are on probation or parole.[45] HI's mission strives for reform through unconditional love and work. As Homeboy's mission statement puts it: "Jobs not Jails"; its logo states: "Nothing Stops a Bullet Like a Job."

As a gang-rehabilitation program, HI's small businesses hire these often difficult-to-place individuals and provide a safe, supportive environment where they learn hard and soft skills, such as showing up on time and taking orders from supervisors, gain work experience, earn a salary to meet their living expenses, and build a resume and a work history. These businesses staffed, in part, by rival ex-gang members who work side-by-side, after completing a job readiness program, include the following four entities.

Homeboy Bakery, HI's original business, founded in 1994, where lead bakers train youths and employ some forty people, turning out more than 3,000 breads and pastries daily that are sold at local farmers' markets and other venues, such as coffeehouses.[46]

Homegirl Café and Catering, begun in 2004, employs some 40 formerly gang-involved young women and men, under a head cook and manager, offering a one-year training program in various aspects of the restaurant and culinary arts industry, including kitchen, hospitality, barista, gardening, and maintenance, and an internship at a partnering restaurant.[47]

Homeboy/Homegirl Merchandise, an on-site and online store, staffed by former gang members and at-risk youth. They learn retailing, including business management, inventory control, sales and promotional skills, by selling casual wear, totes, and other items emblazoned with HI logos and designs.[48]

Homeboy Silkscreen & Embroidery, started in 1996, a thriving business that has employed nearly 500 former gang members, has used silkscreen and embroidery techniques to create designs for clothing and promotional items for more than 2,000 customers.[49]

In 2010, in the midst of the Great Recession, HI, failing to secure its financial base, faced a "near death" crisis, resulting from an increase in costs and a drop in donations that led to massive staff layoffs and the shutting down of many of its services. An infusion of $1.3 million in Los Angeles County funds kept the organization afloat. HI is now on the road to financial recovery.[50]

To create a new revenue stream, in early 2011, HI launched its own line of chips and salsa at a supermarket chain across Southern California.[51] Its salsa is based on Homegirl chef's recipes but is manufactured by a for-profit corporation. Its chips are made by another for-profit corporation. HI receives part of the revenues from the sales of the chips and salsa pursuant to an agreement with the supermarket chain, generating $20,000 a month in profits. The chain waived slotting fees, what manufacturers pay grocery companies to carry a new product, and donated $50,000 to the project.

Looking beyond setting up and operating well-run small businesses, as HI does, where participants learn employment and life skills, both of which are essential to future self-sufficiency and economic independence, and build a work record, successful programmatic efforts turn on implementing a comprehensive approach, paralleling the model of the DCCK's CJT Program. The all-encompassing services HI provides help gang members remove their tattoos, receive mental health and substance abuse and other types of counseling and therapy, and obtain legal services by a full-time on-site attorney. Its educational curriculum includes a charter high school and GED preparation. HI's programs assist clients in finding jobs in private industry, and move away from violence and gang life a process that redirects lives in a positive direction, strengthens an individual and his (or her) family, and by extension, the community at large.

Tattoo removal provided by HI represents a positive technique for assisting youths to step out of gang life and into social integration with the community-at-large.[52] Gang members often have visible tattoos that inhibit their ability to find gainful, legal employment. Tattoo

removal by laser is painful, however, requiring an average of three to ten treatments per tattoo, a process that can take up to one year. Tattoo removal diminishes gang activity and assists releasees, those on probation as well as paroled, ex-prisoners make a successful return to society and the mainstream economy. A point of entry for many HI's clients who come in for tattoo removal and then learn about and take advantage of the other services it offers.

Finally, in its intensive solar panel (photovoltaic) installation training program, HI works with the East Los Angeles Skills Center, a public vocational school, that offers a hands-on program to teach the design, construction, and installation of solar panels.[53] In the HI program, classes are offered for former gang members on parole, among others, in two ten-week cycles, basic and advanced, providing skills training and a pathway to jobs. Program graduates receive nationally recognized certification and assistance with placement. HI provides support services and tutoring in math and literacy to ensure its participants are strong students. HI pays each of its student's tuition and an hourly wage while they are enrolled in the program.

Organizational Structures and Financing of Small Business Established by Nonprofit Organizations

Following the HI model, a nonprofit entity could set up one or more separate for-profit businesses, distinct, but related to its workforce development mission. The for-profit and nonprofit entities must be sufficiently separate to function on their own. Safeguards must also exist so that the for-profit does not receive improper financial benefits from its affiliated nonprofit organization.

To gain funding, beyond what the nonprofit organization can provide, the for-profit entities could approach debt and equity investors on normal, commercial terms. At least two other organizational structures and financing arrangements are possible: a social business model and a Low Profit Limited Liability Company (L3C).

Social Business Model

One possible organizational and financing solution focuses on a concept that Nobel laureate Muhammad Yunus terms a "social business."[54] Yunus's concept involves running a private business not only to earn a profit, but to provide social benefits for those whose lives it touches. He wants to utilize the power of the economic marketplace not only to improve the efficiency of an entity's operations but also to facilitate social improvement. A social business, according to Yunus, is not a charitable organization, but a competitive, self-sustaining enterprise, one that will be financially viable over the long term, neither losing money nor paying dividends. Any profits generated by the enterprise will be plowed back into the entity to support the pursuit of its long-term social goals.

Traditional tax-exempt organizations, in contrast, rely on a stream of donations and public sector subsidies. If these funds fall short (or stop), the good work cannot continue. The need to raise funds from donors and the public sector drains leaders' time and energy. Once a social business is created, it will grow on its own.

Yunus sees social businesses as mainly financed by investors who seek no return (or only a limited return) on their capital in the form of dividends or other types of distributions. Investors would recoup their investment over a long payback period, say ten to twenty years, to reinvest as they wish in the same or a different social (or another) business. It is unclear, however, whether these investors exist in large numbers and whether they will forego a return on their capital.

Low Profit Limited Liability Company

A nonprofit organization's small business could be organized as a L3C.[55] The entity could be branded as "low profit," thereby putting the world on notice that the organization's central purpose focuses on generating social benefit returns, not profit maximization.

To overcome the challenge of financing a social enterprise, an L3C structure would assist in raising capital, especially program-related investments (PRI) from private foundations that do not jeopardize the carrying out of tax exempt purposes and funding by socially minded investors. Other funding sources include "angel" investors, for instance, individuals and pension funds that invest part of their capital in mission-driven entities. L3Cs could also raise funds from various intermediaries, including social venture capital funds, community development financial institutions, social enterprise loan funds, and venture philanthropist organizations.

Nonprofit investors, such as a foundation, would receive compensation through a venture's social outcome. Socially minded investors, individuals, and intermediaries would gain a lower-than-market return for facilitating the entity's socially beneficial mission.

Many details pertaining to L3Cs are, however, beyond the scope of this work. In brief, because of the conduit taxation status of all LLCs, each member is taxed according to its own status, without federal taxation at the entity level. L3C membership agreements can provide for different classes of members, with different rights and powers, unrelated to a membership stake in the venture.

Professionals, including attorneys and accountants, need to create a tool kit of resources for those interested in starting nonprofit maximizing social enterprises, such as social businesses and L3Cs, so interested entities and entrepreneurs can choose and implement the best organizational and financing structure. The tool kit would include relevant checklists and organizational documents. In addition, business consultants and venture capitalists could develop other techniques for meeting the capital challenge quandary. Education and training programs, including conferences and publications, are needed on social enterprises, more generally.[56]

Entrepreneurship Training

In an era of high unemployment and underemployment, making placement with private sector employers difficult, a nonprofit organization's workforce development program could include entrepreneurship and innovation training for those interested in for-profit self-employment. Although not for everyone, entrepreneurship can help unleash the underclass's energy and creativity in a legal manner, offering income and wealth creation through self-employment. In particular, entrepreneurship may appeal to ex-offenders, who previously gained experience in sales and marketing through the drug trade. Often resistant to authority, they may want to be their own bosses. They may take to entrepreneurship, becoming proprietors of successful enterprises able to hire others.

Entrepreneurially oriented programs must be cognizant of state licensing requirement as noted in Chapter 2. In brief, ex-offenders, particularly ex-felons, are often barred from obtaining occupational licenses in a wide variety of fields, on the grounds of their past convictions, even if the offenses are unrelated to their chosen careers.

An extended discussion of a possible entrepreneurship curriculum is, however, beyond the scope of this work. In general terms, entrepreneurship training courses could cover accounting, marketing, negotiating, and similar small business-oriented topics.

Bizdom U, a nonprofit organization founded in 2006, began by focusing on entrepreneurial training in Detroit, and now has expanded to Cleveland.[57] The program seeks to unearth candidates with the right combination of vision, ambition, and risk tolerance, and mold them into innovative, growth-oriented, local business owners, in Detroit or Cleveland. It looks for individuals with a passion for entrepreneurship, demonstrated high achievement in past endeavors, a proven track record as a self-starter, a high level of tenacity and drive, a college degree or technical training (preferred, but not required), leadership or team experience, a desire to accept and apply feedback, and excelling under difficult or stressful conditions.

As originally implemented, groups of some twenty participants met for four months of rigorous training, feedback, and consulting, in reality, a tutorial internship, designed to teach would-be entrepreneurs what they need to know about creating and running successful business enterprises. Mirroring the lifecycle of business development, the program covered business idea development (including recognizing and implementing a successful organizational culture) and business description, feasibility assessment of a proposed business, development of financial projections and an initial sales and marketing strategy, and finalization of a business plan and proposal in preparation to request funding. During this phase, students received free tuition, laptops, BlackBerrys, $1,500 a month living stipend, and hands-on training from Bizdom U's staff members. The program worked with its aspiring entrepreneurs to formulate a business plan for their own locally based businesses.

Those who completed the initial program and developed an approved business plan received funding. The program then offered up to $100,000 for the business described in the plan, incubation workspace, and guidance in launching and operating the firm through eight added months of training, mentoring, and consulting. In return for its initial investment in the start-up, Bizdom U held two-thirds of the entity, the entrepreneur one-third. Once the entrepreneur pays back Bizdom U's investment plus interest, the percentage flips with the student holding a two-thirds stake.

As refined, Bizdom U now offers two distinct programs: Idea Generator and Launch Labs. In the Idea Generator, students with an idea for a new business receive accelerated training to break down an idea and turn it into a business, or go back to the drawing board. Training is offered two to three nights a week and on one or two Saturdays over an eight-week period. If a student's business model proves viable, he or she has the opportunity to seek funding if accepted into Bizdom's Launch Labs.

Those who have completed the Idea Generator Program as well as other entrepreneurs with a well-developed, client-focused, scalable business model, who are ready to build a prototype or a full-fledged business, can seek entry into Bizdom U's Launch Labs programs. If accepted into the program, Bizdom will invest $10,000 plus $4,500 per founder in the business in exchange for an 8 percent equity interest. For three months, the program enables a participant to launch his or her business in a collaborative incubator, receive training in various business functions, such as marketing, and receive coaching and feedback from experienced business, marketing, and technology experts. At the end of an entrepreneur's participation in the Launch Labs program, Bizdom U places him or her in a room with multiple investors to obtain funding needed to take the business to the next level.

After receiving training, start-up entrepreneurs, particularly needy inner city residents, unlike those in the Bizdom's Launch Lab program, face a significant problem—obtaining funding. Because commercial banks find small business lending only marginally profitable as a result of the high transaction costs relative to the amounts lent, a program could couple entrepreneurship training with access to capital to start tiny businesses. This could be done through local microenterprise loan organizations, particularly those requiring participants to save money and invest it wisely to grow their businesses.

These small enterprises, if successful, could provide a reliable way for making a living. It is hard to work for the first few years, but it offers a path for some to economic self-sufficiency, enabling those who can conceive and manage a small business to support themselves and their families and create jobs for others.

Revising Policies to Promote Entrepreneurship

Along with a greater focus on entrepreneurship by nonprofit organizations, must come efforts to usher in a new era of business start-ups leading to the creation of successful firms and jobs, by lifting the burdens imposed by governmental bureaucracies on small businesses. Possibilities for making it easier to start a business include a one-stop public sector website covering all the tax, regulatory, and business license issues. To promote entrepreneurship generally, localities need to reduce, if not eliminate, antibusiness regulations and attitudes. To improve the business climate in America's inner cities, public officials and opinion molders, including clergy, should no longer view profits, in particular, and businesses, in general, with suspicion.

In addition to the regulatory and excessive cost barriers to business formation and operation, oppressive licensing restrictions for various occupations and businesses ought to be reviewed. Granted, that the licensing of some occupations and businesses, such as electricians, is needed to protect health and safety of citizens. However, licensing often serves as a means of protection, enabling existing business owners to keep out upstarts who might offer lower prices or better services, thereby driving up costs to consumers. Licensing also creates huge bureaucracies, including a legion of inspectors to crack down on the unlicensed. Licensing often mandates expensive educational requirements and capstone tests, thereby prohibiting low-income individuals from breaking into a field, at least legally.[58]

Scaling-Up Nonprofit Organizations

After identifying what practices work best and what is making an effective impact, at least locally, it may be difficult to scale-up a successful program to reach a larger number of disconnected individuals and ex-offenders.[59] Often, these efforts cannot be franchised because the capabilities of the founders are crucial to the success of the original entity. Those funding expansion plans must recognize the importance of leadership. Charismatic founders and leaders often offer an inspiring but accurate vision, an experimental mindset, a capacity to live with ambiguity, and an ability to correct a programmatic (or an organizational) course. Also, scaling-up programs may encounter different public sector rules and regulations, a more heterogeneous population, an insufficient service infrastructure, or funding realities that destroy or significantly weaken the attributes that made the original model successful. Nonprofit organizations and their financial backers must begin by identifying what works, sorting the proven from the unproven, and understanding and specifying effective practices. In seeking and achieving scalability, nonprofit organizations and their financial backers must then remain flexible and innovative with respect to unique, specific circumstances and settings. To date, little research exists to help nonprofit entities balance the need to adhere to the original model but adapt to new circumstances.

The Need for Collaboration

It is important to foster collaboration among local like-minded public agencies and nonprofit organizations. In an era of fiscal austerity and ever-tightening budgets, the public and private sectors must work together on common issues. They must collaborate because difficult societal problems, such as those presented by at-risk youth and adults as well as ex-offenders' reentry, cannot be solved by narrowly focused interventions delivered by public sector agencies and nonprofit organizations operating in isolation. Because the issues are interconnected, one agency or entity cannot do it all. Given the need for cooperation, a local or regional group must clarify the limits of separate programs and the potential synergy resulting from collaborative efforts in different areas. Although administratively difficult to patch together the public sector, nonprofit organizations, funders, and employers, models do exist. The National Fund for Workforce Solutions has funded a number of collaborators with strong employer engagement.[60] These arrangements have implemented the range of services low-income, low-skill individuals need to access good jobs in targeted industries.

The Work Place DC (WPDC)[61] exemplifies a fledging public–private partnership in Washington, DC, with complex, multicomponent initiatives and strategies. With many nonprofit organizations active locally in the field of workforce development, competing for funding and having overlapping missions and services, along with numerous public sector agencies, WPDC seeks to integrate and coordinate workforce development programs and services for both local residents and employers. The program strives to engage businesses, government, nonprofit community-based organizations, and individuals to provide a continuum of holistic, comprehensive, high-quality workforce development programs and services to residents in one location, thereby decreasing the number of unemployed and underemployed individuals. It hopes to be the "go to" place for both individuals who want skills enhancement and job placement leading to economic self-sufficiency and an improved quality of life and employers wanting access to high-quality, job-ready employees. WPDC also strives to provide services that support an employee and employer to ensure job retention and job success. For individuals, centralized intake and case management as well as overall program integration is expected to provide each participant with the best chance for employment success. In connecting programs to one another as well as individuals and families to services and supports, and identifying what works to achieve better workforce development outcomes for a community, it likely will find gaps that hopefully can be filled.

Beginning at a single One-Stop location, not the eventual centralized site, WPDC hopes to create a meaningful partnership between the District of Columbia Department of Employment Services and local, nonprofit workforce development service providers. The programs and services that will be offered by partner nonprofit organizations, eventually at one location, include education (Adult Basic Education, GED, and English as Second Language programs), job readiness (such as job etiquette, behavioral change, and anger management), and job training in growth sectors that offer career ladders. The partner nonprofit organizations will also provide case management services to deal with the personal, social, and familial barriers to success as well as various other services, including career counseling and assessment, job placement and retention support, and employment and legal advocacy.

WPDC expects its affiliated organizations to put the common purpose of helping DC residents obtain and retain employment above all else, hopefully with these entities freely sharing information and knowledge. The partner organizations will also strive to establish a common set of quality indicators to evaluate programs and services and identify areas for improvement.

Eventually locating service providers at one location will offer various benefits to the partner organizations. These advantages include economies of scale and increased efficiency derived by combining administrative functions saving each organization time and money; joint fundraising leading to the center applying for larger grants; one organization responsible for intake and case management, eliminating the need for each entity to itself offer these services, and enabling each to do what it does best; and centralized tracking of outputs and outcomes, thereby facilitating the center's overall impact and identifying ways to improve programs and service offerings. A central location will assist clients who otherwise would need to visit many sites scattered throughout an urban area.

At present, much of WPDC's ultimate efforts remain a vision for the future. Largely dependent on public sector funding, hopefully, WPDC can pull together the public and private sectors into a systematic workforce development package to better meet the needs of individuals and employers. Programs must be integrated, aligned toward common goals, and regularly measured to assess the attainment of these objectives.

Given decades of experience with public and nonprofit rehabilitative workforce development programs, the success of these efforts rests on helping those who are motivated to join the mainstream society and for ex-offenders to desist from a life of crime.[62] Substance addicts or others who have not decided to change their ways will not benefit from skills training, among other endeavors. The bottom line: rehabilitation rests on motivating individuals to change their attitudes and behaviors, if not their worldview, as well as evaluate the consequences of their actions. Achieving these motivational objectives depends on each individual. Readiness to change may be easier for adults, not younger individuals. For example, a reanalysis of the results from the National Supported Work Demonstration Project concluded that this program, although having no impact on recidivism for the ex-offender target group, as a whole, had positive results for individuals more than twenty-six years old.[63] These individuals more likely matured sufficiently to desist from crime.

Given the difficulties experienced by rehabilitative programs, the next chapter examines some preventive strategies, focusing on vocational (career and technical) education in public and charter high schools.

Notes

1. D.C. Central Kitchen (DCCK), "Culinary Job Training Program," http://www.dccentralkitchen.org/culinary-job-training.php (accessed November 11, 2010); D.C. Central Kitchen Site Visit Report by Ben Teich, Raisa Shuklov, and David Park, March 25, 2011; DCCK, "Culinary Job Training Program Overview Outline," n.d. See also DeNeen L. Brown, "In the Kitchen, Ingredients for Lives on the Rise," *Washington Post*, May 31, 2009, E3; Neil Irwin, "A Hand Up in a D.C. System Full of Letdowns," *Washington Post*, February 12, 2006, A1.

2. DCCK, "DCCK Mission & Programs Overview," http://www.dccentralkitchen.org/programoverview.php (accessed May 16, 2011) and DCCK, 2009 Internal Revenue Service Form 990, Schedule O.

3. DCCK, "First Helping," http://www.dccentralkitchen.org/firsthelping.php (accessed May 16, 2011); "Meal Distribution," http://www.dccentralkitchen.org/meal-distribution.php (accessed May 16, 2011); "Food Recycling," http://www.dccentralkitchen.org/food-recycling.php (accessed May 16, 2011); "Healthy Returns," http://www.dccentralkitchen.org/healthy-returns.php (accessed May 16, 2011); DCCK, "The Future of Sustainability," Annual Report '09; "20 Years and Moving Forward," Annual Report 2008; 2007 Annual Report, "Combating Hunger, Creating Opportunity"; Annual Report 2006; Annual Report 2005.

   Robert Egger with Howard Yoon, *Begging for Change: The Dollars and Sense of Making Nonprofits Responsive, Efficient, and Rewarding for All*

(New York: HarperCollins, 2004), 34–40, recounted the founding of the D.C. Central Kitchen.

4. Ibid., 40–44, 110–12, narrated the creation of the Culinary Job Training Program.

5. D.C. Central Kitchen Site Visit, n.p.

6. DCCK, "Culinary Job Training Program."

7. DCCK, "Fresh Start, Home," http://www.freshstartcatering.com (accessed May 16, 2011); "The Fresh Start Story," http://www.freshstart catering.com (accessed May 16, 2011). See also Kristen Hinman, "Stars Align for D.C. Central Kitchen's Fresh Start," *Washington Post*, July 20, 2011, E1.

8. D.C. Kitchen Site Visit, n.p.

9. Egger, *Begging For Change*, 98, 112.

10. Interview by author of Mark Goldsmith, August 9, 2011; Getting Out and Staying Out (GOSO), "Who We Are," http://www.gosonyc.org/index.php? (accessed September 12, 2011); "Our History," http://www.gosonyc.org/index.php? (accessed September 12, 2011); "What We Do," http://www.gosonyc.org/index.php? (accessed September 12, 2011); "Our Results," http://www.gosonyc.org/index.php? (accessed September 12, 2011); "GOSO in the Community," http://www.gosonyc.org/index.php? (accessed September 12, 2011); "GOSO Partner Network," http://www.gosonyc.org/index.php? (accessed September 12, 2011); "Welcome to GOSO!" http://www.gosonyc.org/index.php? (accessed May 16, 2011); "History," http://www.gosonyc.org/index.php? (accessed August 4, 2010); "Staff," http://www.gosonyc.org/index.php (accessed August 4, 2010); Carol Hymowitz, "Executives Teach Inmates How to Be Employees," *Wall Street Journal*, March 17, 2008, B7; GOSO Annual 2009–2010 Report, "Getting Out and Staying Out: Re-Entry That Works!"

11. GOSO Annual 2009-2010 Report, n.p.; GOSO, "History."

12. Hymowitz, "Executives Teach."

13. Email to author from Mindy Tarlow, August 12, 2011; Center for Employment Opportunities (CEO), "CEO Model," http://www.ceoworks.org/about/what-we-do> (accessed May 18, 2011); "CEO Theory of Change." http://www.ceoworks.org/about/what-we-do/ceo-model-3 (accessed May 18, 2011), "Our Offices," http://www.ceoworks.org/our-offices (accessed May 18, 2011); "CEO Training," http://www.ceoworks.org/services/nyc-specialized-programs/ceo-training (accessed May 18, 2011); "Mission & Vision," http://www.ceowrks.org/about/what-we-do/mission-vision (accessed March 16, 2011); "Life Skills Education," http://www.ceoworks.org/services/life-skills education (accessed March 16, 2011); "Transitional Jobs," http://www.ceoworks.org/services/transitional-jobs (accessed March 16, 2011); "Job Placement," http://www.ceoworks.org/services/job-placement-information (accessed March 16, 2011); "Post-Placement Services," http://ceoworks.org/services/post-placement services (accessed March 16, 2011); "Parents," http://www.ceoworks.org/services/nyc-specialized programs/parents (accessed March 18, 2011); "Single Stop," http://www.ceoworks.org/services/nyc-specialized-single-stop (accessed May 18, 2011); 2008 Internal Revenue Service (IRS) Form 990. See also Peter Finn, "Successful Job Placement for Ex-Offenders: The Center for Employment Opportunities," U.S. Department of Justice, Office of Justice Programs,

National Institute of Justice, March 1998, NCJ 168102; Dan Bloom and others, "Four Strategies to Overcome Barriers to Employment: An Introduction to Enhanced Services for the Hard-to-Employ," Demonstration and Evaluation Project, MDRC, October 2007, 11–12, 21–24; Cindy Redcross and others, "Transitional Jobs for Ex-Prisoners: Implementation, Two-Year Impacts, and Costs of the Center for Employment Opportunities (CEO) Prisoner Reentry Program," MDRC, August 2009, 13–33.

14.   CEO, "Who We Serve," http://www.ceoworks.org/services/who-we-serve (accessed May 18, 2011).
15.   For background on transitional jobs program and various models see Dan Bloom, "Transitional Jobs: Background, Program Models, and Evaluation Evidence," MDRC, February 2010, 1–26.
16.   Ibid., fn 62 at 42.
17.   Jennifer L. Bryan and others, "CEO's Rapid Rewards Program: Using Incentives to Promote Employment Retention for Formerly Incarcerated Individuals," CEO Learning Institute Report, August 2007, 7 (Figure 4 Retention Outcomes for Different Wage Groups); CEO, "Stakeholder Feedback," http://www.ceoworks.org/resources/impacts/participants-feedback (accessed May 18, 2011).
18.   M. Robin Dion and others, "Reaching All Job-Seekers: Employment Programs for Hard-to-Employ Populations," Mathematical Policy Research, October 1999, 31.
19.   CEO, 2008 IRS Form 990, Schedule O, Part III, Line 4b.
20.   Alana Gunn and Julie Peterson, "CEO's Young Adult Program: Engaging Formerly Incarcerated Young People in the Workforce," CEO Report, October 2007, 6.
21.   Redcross and others, "Transitional Jobs for Ex-Prisoners," ES-6, 47–61.
22.   The statistics in this paragraph are from Ibid., ES-8 (Table 5.1 Two-Year Impacts on Recidivism), 63–76. See also Center for Employment Opportunities and MDRC, "The Power of Work: Comprehensive Prisoner Reentry Program," CEO and MDRC, March 2006, 9–21.
23.   Janine Zweig and others, "Recidivism Effects of the Center for Employment Opportunities (CEO) Program Vary by Former Prisoners' Risk of Reoffending," MDRC, October 2010, 10–13.
24.   CEO, "External Evaluations, CEO Evaluation: Criminal Justice Impacts," http://www.ceowork.org/resources/impacts/external-evaluation (accessed March 16, 2011).
25.   Cindy Redcross and others, "Work After Prison: One-Year Finding from the Transitional Jobs Reentry Demonstration," MDRC, October 2010, iii, ES-2, ES-8, ES-9, ES-12, 67–89, 91–109. See also Christy A. Visher and others, "Ex-Offender Employment Programs and Recidivism: A Meta-Analysis," *Journal of Experimental Criminology* 1, no. 7 (September 2005): 295–315, a quantitative meta-analysis of eight random assignment community employment programs for ex-offenders found no reduction in recidivism; The Joyce Foundation's Transitional Jobs Reentry Demonstration, "Testing Strategies to Help Former Prisoners Find and Keep Jobs and Stay Out of Prison: Implementation and First-Year Results," October 2010; The Joyce Foundation's Transitional Jobs Reentry Demonstration, "Findings: Program Impacts," n.p.; The Joyce Foundation's Transitional Jobs Reentry

Demonstration, "Testing Strategies To Help Former Prisoners Find and Keep Jobs and Stay Out of Prison," July 2009.

Bruce Western, "From Prison to Work: A Proposal for a National Prison Reentry Program," Brookings Institution, Hamilton Project, Discussion Paper 2008-16, December 2008, proposed a federal reentry program with a core element of up to one year of transitional employment for all parolees in need of work. See also John Bouman and Joseph Antolin, "Attacking Poverty by Attacking Chronic Unemployment: A Proposal to Stabilize and Grow the Transitional Jobs Strategy," *Clearinghouse Review* 40, no. 1 (May–June 2006): 105–12.

26.   Safer Foundation (Safer), "History," http://saferfoundation.org/about/ history (accessed May 25, 2011); Safer, 2008 IRS Form 990, Part III 4a; email to author from Veronica Cunningham, December 3, 2011 (Cunningham email). See also Peter Finn, "Chicago's Safer Foundation: A Road Back for Ex-Offenders," U.S. Department of Justice, Office of Justice Programs, National Institute of Justice, June 1998, NCJ 167575; Dion, "Reaching All Job-Seekers," 35–37.

27.   Safer, "Transitional Employment Program," http://saferfoundation.org/ services-programs/transitional-employment-program (accessed May 25, 2011). See also Redcross and others, "Work after Prison," 32–33; Mary Owen, "Work Awaits after Prison," *Chicago Tribune*, May 8, 2009, Chicagoland Extra Section, 4.

28.   Safer, "Sheridan and SWICC," http://saferfoundation.org/services-programs/sheridanswicc (accessed May 25, 2011).

29.   Safer, "2010 Program Update" (Fiscal Year 2009), n.p.

30.   Safer, "Youth Education Program," http://saferfoundation.org/services-programs/youth-education-program (accessed May 25, 2011). See also Ron Tonn, "Turning the Tables: The Safer Foundation's Youth Empowerment Program," *Corrections Today* 61, no. 1 (February 1999): 76, 78.

31.   Cunningham email. See also Safer, 2008 IRS Form 990, Part III 4b.

32.   Sheila Maquire and others, "Job Training that Works: Findings from the Sectoral Employment Impact Study," Public/Private Ventures In Brief, Issue 7, May 2009. See also Anne Roder with Carol Clymer and Laura Wyckoff, "Targeting Industries, Training Workers and Improving Opportunities: The Final Report from the Sectoral Employment Initiative," Public/Private Ventures, 2008, 19–34; Lily Zandniapour and Maureen Conway, "Gaining Ground: The Labor Market Progress of Participants of Sectoral Employment Development Programs," SEDLP Research Report No. 3, Aspen Institute, Economic Opportunities Program, February 2002, 16–25, 28–36.

33.   Harry J. Holzer and others, "Employer Demand for Ex-Offenders: Recent Evidence from Los Angeles," March 2003, 11–12.

34.   Beyond the scope of this work are federally funded child care programs, particularly the Child Care and Development Block Grants. See Hannah Matthews, "Child Care Assistance in 2009: Spending Update," Center for Law and Social Policy (CLASP), March 2011. Evaluations of child care funding include U.S. Government Accountability Office, "Child Care and Development Fund: Undercover Tests Show Five State Programs are Vulnerable to Fraud and Abuse," September 2010, GAO-10-1062; Hannah Matthews, "Child Care Assistance: A Program that Works," CLASP,

January 23, 2009; Jennifer Mezey and others, "Unfinished Agenda; Child Care for Low-Income Families Since 1996: Implications for Federal and State Policies," CLASP, March 2002.

35. Beyond the scope of this work, eighty federal programs in eight federal departments provided funding for transportation services for the transportation disadvantaged in fiscal year 2010. According to the U.S. Government Accountability Office, transportation programs overlap one another with a fragmentation existing among agencies providing these transportation services. Opportunities to Reduce Potential Duplication in Government Programs, Save Tax Dollars, and Enhance Revenue, March 2011, GAO-11-318SP, 134–38.

36. See generally, Jean E. Rhodes, *Stand by Me: The Risks and Rewards of Mentoring Today's Youth* (Cambridge: Harvard University, 2002); Jean E. Rhodes and others, "A Model for the Influence of Mentoring Relationships on Youth Development," *Journal of Community Psychology* 34, no. 6 (November 2006): 691–707. See also Susan Jekielek and others, "Mentoring Programs and Youth Development," Child Trends, January 2002; Shawn Bauldry, "Positive Support: Mentoring and Depression among High-Risk Youth," Public/Private Ventures, June 2006.

37. For a summary of the impact of mentoring programs on ex-offenders see Shawn Bauldry and others, "Mentoring Formerly Incarcerated Adults: Insights from the Ready4Work Reentry Initiative," Public/Private Ventures, Field Report Series, January 2009; Wendy S. McClanahan, "Mentoring Ex-Prisoners in the Ready4Work Reentry Initiative," Public/Private Ventures, Preview, March 2007; Elaine A. Bleichman and Jedediah M. Bopp, "Juvenile Offenders," in *Handbook of Youth Mentoring*, ed. David L. DuBois and Michael J. Karcher (Thousand Oaks, CA: Sage, 2005), 457–59. Research studies include Elaine A. Blechman and others, "Can Mentoring or Skill Training Reduce Recidivism? Observational Study with Propensity Analysis," *Prevention Science* 1, no. 3 (September 2006): 139–55. See generally, Gary Walker, "Mentoring Policies and Politics," Public/Private Ventures, P/PV Brief, October 2007.

38. Key components of an effective mentoring program are summarized in Franklin Schargel and Jay Smink, *Strategies to Help Solve our School Dropout Problem* (Larchmont, NY: Eye on Education, 2001), 88–94. See also Renata Cobbs Fletcher and Jerry Sherk with Linda Jucovy, "Mentoring Former Prisoners: A Guide for Reentry Programs," Public/Private Ventures, November 2009; Shawn M. Coyne and others, "Mentoring for Results: Accountability at the Individual, Program, Community, and Policy Levels," in *Handbook of Youth Mentoring*, 546–60.

39. For an example of the difficulties the Harlem Children's Zone encountered because of its dependency on previously steady donors when those revenues dried up, as they did during the Great Recession, see Mike Spector, "Bear Market for Charities," *Wall Street Journal*, January 24–25, 2009, A1.

40. Shelia B. Rossman, "Case-Managed Reentry and Employment: Lessons from the Opportunity to Succeed Program," *Justice Research and Policy* 5, no. 2 (Fall 2003): 75–100, at 86–87.

41. For an analysis of seven programs that acquired cars and made them available to low-income workers see Carolyn D. Hayden and Bronwyn

Mauldin, "On the Road: Car Ownership as an Asset Building Strategy for Reduce of Transportation Related Barriers to Work," National Economic Development and Law Center, 2002, 10–16. Best practices for nonprofits that want to create car ownership programs are discussed in Ibid., 2, 17–20.

42. Email to author from Chris Callison, September 16, 2011; Wheels of Success, Inc., "Program Summary," http://www.wheelsofsuccess.org/about-us/program-summary.html (accessed March 29, 2010); "Eligibility Guidelines," http://www.wheelsofsuccess.org/our-work/index.html (accessed March 29, 2010). See also Sarah Hutchins, "Nonprofit Provides Cars for Struggling Families," *St. Petersburg Times*, September 4, 2010, B1; "Local Women Gets Wheels of Success," *tbnweekly.com*, September 7, 2009, http://www.wheelsofsuccess.org/news/news/090709-TBN-Weekly.html (accessed April 5, 2010); Mary Shedden, "Wheels Helps Drive Worker Success," *Tampa Tribune*, April 28, 2007, 1; Christina Rexrode, "Here's a Key to Stability," *St. Petersburg Times*, March 25, 2007, F2; Judy Hill, "Wheels Program Gets Needy Rolling," *Tampa Tribune*, September 21, 2006, Baylife Section 1; Judy Hill, "Helping Those Who Need Reliable Cars," *Tampa Tribune*, January 29, 2004, Baylife Section 1.

43. Homeboy Industries (HI), "About us," http://www.homeboy-industries.org/what.php (accessed May 18, 2011); "Why We Do It," http://www.homeboy-industries.org/why.php (accessed May 18, 2011); "History," http://www.homeboy-industries.org/history.php (accessed May 18, 2011); "What We Do," http://www.homeboy-industries.org/what-we-do.php (accessed May 18, 2011); "Services," http://www.homeboy-industries.org/services.php (accessed May 18, 2011); "Overview," http://www.homeboy-industries.org/overview-shop-businesses.php (accessed March 30, 2010); HI clients have a 20 percent recidivism rate. Email to author from Edgar Gonzalez, October 11, 2011. Gregory Boyle, *Tattoos on the Heart: The Power of Boundless Compassion* (New York: Free Press, 2010), 4–12, described the founding and growth of Homeboy Industries and one of its businesses, Homeboy Bakery. See also Gregory Boyle, "Street Priest," *Guideposts* 65, no. 12 (February 2011): 60–64.

44. For background on gangs see Terence P. Thornberry and others, *Gangs and Delinquency in Developmental Perspective* (New York: Cambridge, 2003), 42–54, 105–8 (gang membership and delinquency), 109–11 (drug involvement), 164–76 (crime and disorders). See also Beth M. Huebner and others, "Gangs, Guns and Drugs: Recidivism among Serious, Young Offenders," *Criminology & Public Policy* 6, no. 2 (May 2007): 187–221.

45. Alexandra Zavis, "Homeboy Industries Gets $1.3-million County Contract," *Los Angeles Times*, September 15, 2010, AA4.

46. HI, "Homeboy Bakery," http://www.homeboy-industries.org/homeboy-bakery.php (accessed May 18, 2011). See also Tami Abdollah, "A New Bakery Renews Old Hope"; Kate Linthicum, "Homeboy Diner Feeds Two Needs," *Los Angeles Times*, October 1, 2007, B1.

47. HI, "Homegirl Café and Catering," http://www.homegirlcafe.org/about-us (accessed May 25, 2011). See also Kurt Streeter, "Gangs on Back Burner at the Homegirl Cafe," *Los Angeles Times*, September 5, 2005, B1; In June

2011, HI opened a satellite diner, Homeboy Diner, modeled after Homegirl Café, in the Los Angeles City Hall. Kate Linthicum, "Homeboy Dinner Feeds Two Needs," *Los Angeles Times*, June 11, 2011, AA1.

48. HI, "Homeboy/Homegirl Merchandise," http://www.homeboy-industries-org/homeboy-merchandise.php (accessed May 18, 2011).

49. HI, "Homeboy Silkscreen & Embroidery," http://www.homeboy-industries. org/silkscreen-embroidery.php (accessed May 18, 2011).

50. Zavis, "Homeboy Industries Gets $1.3-million County Contract." See also Hector Becerra, "Boyle and Homeboy Were Living a Paradox," *Los Angeles Times*, May 15, 2010, AA1; Hector Becerra, "L.A.'s Homeboy Industries Lays Off Most of Its Employees," *Los Angeles Times*, May 14, 2010, A1.

51. Betty Hallock, "Chips, Salsa and Purpose," *Los Angeles Times*, February, 17, 2011, E1; Jerry Hirsch, "Ralphs Takes a Chance on Salsa from At-Risk Youths," *Los Angeles Times*, October 9, 2009, B2.

52. HI, "Ya'Stuvo (that's enough, I'm done with that) Tattoo Removal," http:// www.homeboy-industries.org/tattoo-removal.php (accessed March 30, 2010). The Renova International Foundation tattoo removal program removes gang tattoos from those in prison, jail, on parole or probation. The program organizes volunteer dermatologists to perform the removal operations. On tattoo removal generally see Laura Johannes, "Home Remedies to Fade Your Heart on Your Sleeve," *Wall Street Journal*, February 8, 2011, D2.

53. Miriam Jordan, "A New Gang Comes to Los Angeles," *Wall Street Journal*, February 14, 2009, A1.

54. Muhammad Yunus with Karl Webber, *Creating a World without Poverty: Social Business and the Future of Capitalism* (New York: PublicAffairs, 2007), 21–28.

55. In-depth discussions of a Low Profit Limited Liability Company organizational structure and finance include Thomas Kelly, "Law and Choice of Entity on the Social Enterprise Frontier," *Tulane Law Review* 84, no. 2 (December 2009): 337–77; Dennise Bayona and Ken Milani, "The L3C Low-Profit Limited Liability Company: Investment Option for Societal Impact," *Practical Tax Strategies* 86, no. 2 (February 2011): 66–71. Another corporate firm, B corporation (Benefit corporation), enables social entrepreneurs to combine making a profit with "doing good" and requires corporate directors to pursue a broad set of social and environmental objectives in addition to profits. Hannah Clark, "A New Kind of Company: B Corporations Worry about Stakeholders, Not Just Shareholders," *INC* 29, no. 7 (July 2007): 23–24; Ben Gose, "Nonprofits Worry about California's Efforts to Create Social Business Units," *Chronicle of Philanthropy*, May 19, 2011, 9. See also Stephanie Strom, "A Quest for Hybrid Companies That Profit, but Can Tap Charity," *New York Times*, October 13, 2011, B1.

56. Michael Chertok and others, "The Funding Gap," *Stanford Social Innovation Review* 6, no. 2 (Spring 2008): 44–51, at 50–51.

57. Letter to the author from Ross Sanders, September 1, 2011; Bizdom U, "FAQs," http://www.bizdom.com/program/faq (accessed September 12, 2011); "About the Program," http://www.bizdom.com/program (accessed September 12, 2011); "Our Entrepreneurs Invest," http://www.bizdom.

com/program/entrepreneurers (accessed September 12, 2011); "Business Development and Planning," http://www.bizdom.com/program/business-development-funding (accessed September 12, 2011); "What is Bizdom U?" http://www.bizdom.com (accessed May 18, 2011); "FAQs," http://www.bizdom.com/program/faq (accessed May 18, 2011); "About the Program," http://www.bizdom.com/program (accessed March 3, 2011); "We Invest," http://www.bizdom.com/program/invest (accessed March 3, 2011); "Our Entrepreneurs Invest," http://www.bizdom.com/program/entrepreneurs (accessed March 3, 2011); "Business Development and Planning," http://www.bizdom.com/program/business-development-funding (accessed March 3, 2011); "The Launch Pad," http://www.bizdom.com/program/the-launch (accessed March 3, 2011). See also Pamela Ryckman, "Fostering Entrepreneurs, and Trying to Revive a City," *New York Times*, June 24, 2010, B6; Jon Swartz, "Thanks to Bizdom U, Detroit Builds Entrepreneurs, Too," *USA Today*, April 20, 2009, B1; Michelle Jarboe, "Gilbert's Bizdom U to Train Aspiring Entrepreneurs Here," *Plain Dealer* (Cleveland, OH), October 29, 2010, C1; Jennifer Youssef, "Bizdom U Grads Set to Go Local," *Detroit News*, September 29, 2008, A8; Tom Walsh, "Entrepreneurs Ready to Get City's Economy Rolling," *Detroit Free Press*, July 31, 2008, 1; Jennifer Youssef, "A Spark for Startups," *Detroit News*, June 15, 2007, C1; Jennifer Youssef, "Bizdom U Gets Ideas off the Ground," *Detroit News*, December 18, 2006, C1; Shenna Harrison, "Bizdom U. Set to Teach Next Gen of Startups," *Crain's Detroit Business*, November 13, 2006, 1.

In 2009, Goldman Sachs announced a half-billion program to help 10,000 existing small business owners working predominantly in "underserved" markets with at least four full-time employees, in business for at least two years, and having annual revenues from $150,000 to $4 million per year in their most recent fiscal year. Over five years, Goldman Sachs will spend $200 million on education and training programs and funnel $300 million to community-development financial institutions. Making debt and equity investments, these institutions serve economically disadvantaged communities that historically have had difficulty accessing capital. Delivering training through community colleges, among other institutions, to date, the program has yielded modest but tangible results with five hundred business owners in New York City, Houston, New Orleans, Chicago, Long Beach, and Los Angeles completing a twenty-week curriculum. Goldman Sachs, 10,000 Small Businesses, Fact Sheet, n.d. See also Mike Spector, "Small Businesses Turn to Goldman," *Wall Street Journal*, November 19, 2009, C5; Steve Garmhausen, "Goldman Lends $500M-gradually," *Crain's New York Business*, May 24, 2010, 9; Dyan Machan, "Goldman Sachs + Warren Buffet + $500 million = Not Many Jobs Yet," *SmartMoney* 21, no. 1 (January 2012): 44.

58. Stephanie Simon, "A License to Shampoo," *Wall Street Journal*, February 7, 2011, A1; Chip Mellor and Dick Carpenter, "Want Jobs? Cut Local Regulations," *Wall Street Journal*, July 28, 2011, A15; Sara Burrows, "Proposed Occupational Licensing Laws Target Entrepreneurs!" *Carolina Journal*, July 2011, 5.

59. For a syntheses of key structures that must be in place before a nonprofit considers widescale republication see Geri Summerville with Becca Raley,

"Laying a Solid Foundation: Strategies for Effective Program Replication," Public/Private Ventures, July 2009. See also Brandon C. Welsh and others, "When Early Crime Prevention Goes to Scale: A New Look at the Evidence," *Preventive Science* 11, no. 2 (June 2010): 115–25; Delbert S. Elliott and Sharon Milhalic, "Issues in Disseminating and Replicating Effective Prevention Programs," *Preventive Science* 5, no. 1 (March 2004): 47–53; Felip Gozález Castro and others, "The Cultural Adaptation of Prevention Interventions: Resolving Tensions between Fidelity and Fit," *Preventive Science* 5, no. 1 (March 2004): 41–45; Thomas E. Backer, "The Failure of Success: Challenges of Disseminating Effective Substance Abuse Prevention Programs," *Journal of Community Psychology* 28, no. 3 (May 2000): 363–73.

60. Barbara Baran and others, "Implementing the National Fund for Workforce Solutions: The Baseline Evaluation Report," National Fund for Workforce Solutions, December 2, 2009; Barbara Baran and others, "Implementing the National Fund for Workforce Solutions: Second Annual National Evaluation Report," National Fund for Workforce Solutions, May 2010. See also Colin Taylor, "Employer Engagement in the National Fund for Workforce Solutions," National Fund for Workforce Solutions, January 2011.

61. The Work Place DC: Concept Paper, Draft, August 30, 2010; The Work Place DC, 2009–2010 Accomplishments.

62. See, e.g., Shawn Bushway, "Reentry and Prison Work Programs, Urban Institute Reentry Roundtable, Employment Dimensions of Poverty: Understanding the Nexus between Prisoner Reentry and Work," May 2003, 8–9.

63. Christopher Uggen, "Work as a Turning Point in the Life Course of Criminals: A Duration Model of Age, Employment, and Recidivism," *American Sociological Review* 65, no. 4 (August 2000): 529–46.

4

Intermediate-Term Preventive Strategies, Programs, and Policies to Facilitate Skills Training in High Schools and Alternative Venues

Some people prefer to work with their hands or toil outdoors; they do not like being stuck at a desk every workday. Often they want to provide something tangible if not each day, then during the workweek. They want to make a concrete difference in other's lives. They want to find satisfaction in being good, if not excellent, but not mediocre, at what they do for a living. For them, satisfaction can from come from nonacademic excellence. Thus, skill-based high school and other alternative training options may provide better opportunities for them in the job market, in terms of employment possibilities and wages.

Demand exists for skilled workers, with the need increasing faster than the supply, even following the Great Recession. Vocational high school and alternative programs do not relegate students to less financially and emotionally rewarding careers. These programs do not limit job opportunities; rather they widen access to positions, particularly for black males, who see potentially rewarding alternatives to dropping out of academically oriented high schools. By providing links to employers, these programs enable black men access to good jobs that are less dependent on informal contacts generated through one's network of relatives and friends.

To meet the demand, vocational (career and technical [CTE]) education prepares students who enter the workforce directly from high school with marketable skills and knowledge. The skills and knowledge developed in high school CTE classes and programs will hopefully offer a road to future success in the workplace.

After summarizing the benefits of a high school diploma, this chapter examines the federal funding for vocational education. It then presents a rationale for a vocational education strategy and an overview of CTE today in the United States, focusing on the current benefits of a vocational education and the promise offered by career academies. After offering educational policy recommendations for public high schools, one charter school program and a nonhigh school alterative are examined.

The chapter urges that over the next three to five years, the inter- mediate-term, policymakers, donors, and social entrepreneurs place greater emphasis on vocational training in high schools and alterna- tive venues, and partner with local employers to give students work experiences, such as internships. This approach will help provide more opportunities for young people, especially black males, to develop their skill levels. Hands-on high school and alternative educational programs will help facilitate careers that are (and will likely be) in demand.

The Benefits of a High School Diploma

Studies point to the benefit of a high school diploma. Generally speaking, high school graduation is associated with an increased likelihood of employment and higher income levels in adulthood.[1] This, in turn, has economic advantages in the form of additional tax revenues.[2]

Beyond economic advantages to individuals and the public, the benefits of high school graduation accrue especially to African- Americans. A high school diploma may help keep black men out of trouble. The likelihood of incarceration drops by more than 40 percent among black high school graduates compared to those who only make it to the tenth or eleventh grade. Society also benefits. A 1 percent increase in the high school graduation rate of all men ages twenty to sixty would save the nation as much as $1.4 billion per year that would otherwise be spent in keeping high school dropouts behind bars.[3]

As indicated in Chapter 1 about 50 percent of inner city black males do not graduate from high school. The one-size-fits-all, academically oriented high school education, currently in vogue, does not, however, fit all. The failure of black males in the modern American economy and mainstream society is, in part, a failure of education. If young black males did better academically, fewer would drop out before finishing high school. As a result, their prospects for employment would be better, fewer would succumb to the life of the streets, and to drug dealing that leads to mass incarceration. Because students differ in their learning styles and goals, policymakers, funders, and social entrepreneurs need to create more options, specifically, CTE, that incline more students to stay in and graduate from high school.

Federal Funding for Vocational Education

Based on the importance of job-oriented training, the federal government has a long history of supporting vocational education, going back to the Smith-Hughes Act of 1917,[4] which provided funds to the states to prepare youths for occupations not requiring postsecondary education. With the enactment of the Vocational Education Act of 1963,[5] federal legislation has specified basic requirements, while giving state and local funding recipients considerable flexibility in meeting congressional mandates. In exchange for increased programmatic flexibility at the state and local levels in preparing students for productive employment, recognizing that vocational education programs are best administered by those nonfederal entities having better positions to make educational decisions, federal enactments have placed an increasing emphasis on accountability.

A 1983 report, *A Nation at Risk*,[6] set in motion the accountability movement that led to academic standards reform in many states and culminated at the federal level in the enactment of the No Child Left Behind Act of 2001. In 1984, Congress passed the Carl D. Perkins Vocational Education Act[7] requiring states, as a condition of receiving federal grant funds, to improve their vocational education programs. Together with a new focus on academics based on the premise that many more students could achieve high academic standards, came requirements that vocational programs must be academically rigorous but also offer real-world relevance.

In the 1990s, CTE emerged in place of traditional vocational education. The change in terminology reflected the new skills students needed in the competitive global economy.

In 1998, when Congress reauthorized the Perkins Act,[8] it bolstered academic standards, mandated updating and strengthening the CTE curriculum, and made high schools more accountable for student performance and programmatic expenditures. The 1998 reauthorization included for the first time a requirement that CTE programs demonstrate that their students were meeting the same academic standards as other high school students.

The latest embodiment of federal efforts, the Carl D. Perkins Career and Technical Education Improvement Act of 2006,[9] provides nearly $1.4 billion in federal funding annually for CTE programs nationwide through 2012. The 2006 act contains an increased focus on academic rigor for and achievement by CTE students; it also strives to improve state and local accountability and strengthen the connections between secondary and postsecondary education. In return for continued federal support, Congress wants to see data on student achievement and progress, in terms of various performance measures, such as tests, projects, and portfolios, established by the states.

Today, a combination of federal, state, local, and private funds supports CTE programs. Most funding comes from state and local education budgets, with federal financial support of $1.4 billion annually remaining basically constant at about 10 percent of aggregate funding.[10] Although the federal share of funding for CTE is relatively small, federal mandates help drive programmatic changes in high school workforce preparation at the state and local levels.

A Vocational Education Strategy: A Rationale

The nation needs to encourage black males to graduate from high school and, at the same time, to receive a meaningful education, so that they are not functionally illiterate. The public and nonprofit workforce development strategies and programs aimed at disconnected youth and adults analyzed in Chapters 2 and 3 of this work represent a second-best approach. In comparison to second chance, rehabilitative public sector training programs targeting high school dropouts, such as Job Corps, Job Start, and the youth training program previously funded by the federal Job Training Partnership Act, one cost-benefit analysis concluded, "it is much better to prevent at-risk students from dropping out and to induce them to occupation-specific education at their local high school or a regional tech center."[11]

Yet, today, high schools using a "one-size-fits-all" model encourage nearly everyone to go on to a two-or-four-year college, even community college for those with weak academic records. The supposed higher status and earning power of college-educated middle managers and administrators as well as white-collar knowledge workers fuels this approach, leading to current educational policy emphasizing academic skills and standards. College is seen as the ticket to the middle class and living the "American Dream."

Guidance counselors continue to steer as many high school students as possible to the college prep/academic track,[12] forcing them to take a foreign language and study calculus, even if they do not belong there and are bored. They trumpet the message that if you want to succeed in life, you must go to college. Guidance counselors seem reluctant to discourage almost any student from pursuing a route to a college education. They do little to combat the negative images often associated with occupational training during high school years.

However, while motivating students to do academic work in high school is critical, many do not like the college prep track or classrooms. As a result, they do not work hard and consequently they do not do well. Boredom is endemic in American high schools. In 2009, 42,754 students from 103 high schools in 27 states participated in the High School Survey of Student Engagement.[13] Two out of three respondents were bored at least every day in class in high school. About one out of six students (17 percent) were bored in every class. Of the students who claimed they were bored, more than four out of five (81 percent) noted a reason for their boredom as "material was not interesting." About two out of five students (42 percent) claimed that the lack of relevance of the material caused their boredom. A lack of instructional interaction played a role in students' boredom. More than one-third of the respondents (35 percent) were bored due to "no interaction with teacher."

Bored, uncurious, lazy, and feeling the material is irrelevant, students, especially those lacking impulse control, often become unruly and disruptive. They manifest an antiachievement disposition and a counterproductive attitude towards education.[14]

Besides linguistic (language and the information conveyed by language) and logical-mathematical (abstractions, logic, numbers) intelligence, two indispensable keys to academic success, we now know there are multiple intelligences, including body-kinesthetic (physical skills), musical, interpersonal (effective interacting with others), intrapersonal (knowing oneself and effectively using that knowledge), and spatial (mental visualization and manipulation of objects).[15] Thus, a need exists to assess the nonacademic (nonlinguistic and nonlogical-mathematical) abilities of students and direct them to fields which they reasonably could succeed; something they enjoy doing and can learn how to do it well. For those not suited to a career requiring intense academic coursework and are work-bound, rather than college-bound, we need to help them acquire the skills to make a living. That often means vocational training in high school.

Although many white-collar parents would prefer that their offspring pursue an academic track and do not want their children regressing, at least as they see it, back to the working-class status, in reality, America lacks enough skilled workers. It is important to recognize that vo-tech education will not trap people in low-wage, dead-end jobs.

The Great Recession has taught us some important educational policy lessons. A mismatch may exist between college graduates, especially new graduates, and available starter jobs and ultimate careers.[16] Rather than pointing everyone to college in preparation for life as a knowledge worker, a demand exists in the United States for wide variety of skilled workers and craftspeople—plumbers, masons, welders, cabinetmakers, carpenters, and auto mechanics—those whom we daily depend on to unclog toilets and fix cars. Many of these in-demand jobs do not require a college degree or even some form of higher education.[17] Although the unemployment rates for high school graduates (and dropouts) are much higher than those for college graduates, the skilled trades offer a good living to those who don the blue collar and work with their hands and minds.[18] A dichotomy does not exist between work knowledge and manual work. In addition to earning a good income, they receive intrinsic rewards from mastering a challenging skill that yields tangible results. Essential "blue collar" workers are in demand, although they may not have the same prestige as white-collar employees. Top plumbers can find jobs even in the depth of a recession; mediocre middle managers often cannot. Manufacturing firms cannot find competent machinists and repair technicians. There are not enough mechanics. The on-site or in-person services of skilled workers cannot be outsourced abroad or performed by machines or robots.

Rather than sitting in a cubicle and doing depersonalized, abstract office work, that is, more often than not, characterized by hollow, rote tasks that may leave little room for thinking, many want to experience and see a direct impact of their own actions in the world, using their own hands. Daily and weekly they want to know that they have done something that is right in front of them. In contrast, office workers may find it difficult to see any results from their daily or weekly efforts that are filled with budget projections and planning meetings.

Vocational (career and technical) education programs in high schools provide skills training linking the classroom with hands-on experiences.[19] American educational policy, however, moved in a different direction.

Going back some thirty years, the 1983 report of The National Commission on Excellence in Education[20] led to a de-emphasis on vocational education in educational policy circles. Many states increased their academic requirements for high school graduation and introduced minimum competency tests for obtaining a high school diploma.[21] High schools came to emphasize an academic orientation, largely ignoring any potential connections to the general world of work or any specific careers. States also sought to integrate academic and vocational courses, encourage vocational education students to take additional higher level academic classes, both in number and rigor, and generally upgrade content of vocational programs.[22]

Responding to employers' increased knowledge and skill demands, high schools also changed the types of CTE courses offered. Not unexpectedly, the numbers of health care and computer-related occupational courses soared, while courses in traditional fields, such as auto mechanics, declined. Also, those students taking three or more courses in a specific occupational field, so-called occupational concentrators, were required to take an increased number of academic courses, thereby raising the percentage of occupational concentrators attending college. High schools accomplished the increase in the academic courses taken by raising the number of courses required and reducing the number of introductory vocational courses, particularly typing and keyboarding. Students generally maintained their vocational education orientation by increasing the total number of credits they earned.

High School Career and Technical Education Today

Most U.S. high schools offer some vocational (CTE) courses and programs.[23] Students typically take these at one of the nation's comprehensive public high schools that enroll most high school students. In 2002, about 88 percent of these public comprehensive high schools offered specific labor market preparation in at least one program, either on-site or off-site.[24] The occupation fields offered vary widely, including business, marketing, health care, information technology, hospitality, construction, and transportation, with the most common, business and information technology.[25]

For most high school graduates, their use of CTE courses is broad, not narrow.[26] Most (58 percent) earn credits in more than one occupational area. They do not concentrate their courses, with 55 percent of the occupational credit-earners not concentrating in one occupational area. Although most public high school graduates (92 percent) from the class of 2005 took at least one occupational course, only about one in five (21 percent) of these graduates completed an occupation concentration, earning three or more credits in three-year-long courses in one occupational program.[27]

In many urban school districts, students may attend a full-day vocational public (or charter) high school. About 1,900 CTE high schools offer concentrated occupational studies and related academic course work in one facility.[28] Those students who attend schools that do not offer occupation-specific CTE or who want to pursue a field of study not offered at their local high school can spend part of their school day at one of about 1,200 (1,191) regional vocational–technical centers, while continuing to take academic courses at their home high school.[29]

The Benefits of a Vocational Education Strategy

Students pursuing a vocational education program in high school receive three benefits: first, enhanced motivation resulting in an increased likelihood of high school graduation; second, teachers and others serving as mentors; and third, doing better in job market postgraduation in terms of employment rates and wages in comparison to those who drop out of high school.

Improving High School Graduation Rates

Although some conclude that mixed evidence exists on whether participation in vocational education reduces the likelihood of dropping out of high school,[30] most studies point to the positive, but modest, impact of CTE programs on high school graduation rates. One analysis of international cross-sectional data found that nations enrolling a "large" percentage of upper-level high school students in vocational programs significantly raised school attendance rates. As a result, these counties increased their high school graduation rates.[31]

Looking at U.S. statistics, students who add CTE courses to their high school curriculum, particularly a middle-range mix consisting of taking one CTE course for every two academic courses, reduced the risk of dropping out, at least for those not too old when they entered the ninth grade.[32] Other research indicated that any participation in CTE courses decreased the dropout rate of noncollege-bound youngsters by about 6 percent.[33]

High school graduation rates improve because CTE courses and programs enable students with different learning styles to grasp academic courses, enhance student motivation, and offer students hands-on experience with work-based learning complementing the technical and academic components. CTE coursework clarifies the value of academic classes by specifying the knowledge and skills needed to succeed in careers of interest, leading students to see the enhanced benefits associated with staying in high school and graduating. CTE courses build on the existence of different learning styles, with many high school students preferring practical application to abstract concepts. These students do better when learning has concrete application; they like using concepts to deal with specific situations.

CTE teaching relies on contextual learning, in the classroom, laboratories, and the workplace. For some students, applying academic and technical knowledge and skills to the real world and being able to see how their education relates to the world of work makes the entire curriculum more interesting and thus more motivating than the traditional academic offerings of English, foreign language, science, math, and history. A career focus gives some students a better sense of direction, thereby motivating them to both achieve and remain in high school. This is important for those who learn best by doing.

Career-focused high school education serves as a useful pedagogical role in helping some students, especially the more practically oriented, master academic subjects. Teaching academic subjects in a real-world context helps these students see the relevance of education to their careers. Making the learning of academic subjects relevant to student concerns helps increase motivation. Students find a practical application of academic materials in the CTE courses. For example, a hospitality student uses a simple algebraic equation to turn a recipe for four people into one for forty. Furthermore, academic skills, such as math, reading, writing, and problem-solving, are subtly taught without instilling fear in students who often encountered negative, past experiences with academic subjects. Teaching academic concepts in the context of real-world problems helps some students value what they learn, thereby increasing their interest, effort, and engagement more than a program of just traditional academic classes. Job-specific terminology and realistic work situations motivate students to apply themselves even to academic courses. Student motivation represents a critical input, central to improving high school education outcomes, particularly graduation rates. Because students identify the skills and knowledge needed to succeed in the workplace through their CTE coursework, the curriculum provides an impetus to stay in school to gain these benefits.

Students, who would otherwise fail to see a link between their academic courses and their future careers, are often weary of school by the ninth or tenth grade. One poll of California ninth and tenth graders enrolled in public schools found that six in ten respondents (61 percent) lacked the motivation to succeed in school. Of those students, about 90 percent (89 percent) said they would be more engaged in their education if classes helped them acquire knowledge and skills relevant to their future careers.[34] CTE courses and programs resonate with many of these students.

CTE courses typically include supervised laboratory instruction that follows classroom work. In the laboratory, concepts are applied in the context of typical jobs. Laboratory instruction, using problem-solving and hands-on experience, helps ensure that the knowledge and skills students learn are relevant to and usable in work-related situations.

In addition to the technical component, which delivers industry-related knowledge and skills, and academic subjects, which teach concepts in an occupational context, most CTE programs offer a work-based learning component. These work-based programs enable students to enroll in job shadowing and internships that reinforce classroom and laboratory learning and help develop on-the-job skills. The most common type of work-based learning experience is job shadowing. This approach teaches students about a job by having them follow the schedule of an individual who holds that position.[35]

Internships involve placing students for a specified time period in a work setting. In addition to observing employees, students participate in appropriate work routines and tasks under skilled workers so as to gain first-hand experience in various aspects of a career. Students further develop their skills and apply what they have learned in school to actual work tasks. Internships are typically a capstone experience in students' senior year in high school.

In short, out-of-class, supervised work experiences, such as internships, at worksites reinforce classroom and laboratory learning. These real-life work opportunities are experiential, requiring students to reflect on and evaluate what happened. Students present what they learned, what worked (and did not work), what knowledge or skills they applied, and what they liked (or did not like) about the experience. Learning by doing at the side of an experienced worker help students unlock the value and benefits of learning.

Mentorships

CTE programs provide students with a second benefit, namely, mentoring that serves as a CTE hallmark. Emphasizing independent and small group work, CTE courses enable teachers to develop meaningful, sustaining relationships with students. CTE students also develop positive relationships with stable, supportive adults in the broader community through internships, for example. Connecting youth with caring adults—mentors—provides a constructive strategy to lessen negative peer influences that may encourage gang membership, drug use, and crime, among other detrimental behaviors. The intervention by someone paid to offer expert advice, such as a mentor who provides sustenance of the most personal kind, is often critical in a student's life. Human contact can make a profound difference. According to one survey of high school dropouts, "These young people craved one-to-one attention from their teachers, and when they received it, they remembered it making a difference."[36]

As discussed in Chapter 1, black teen, inner city males often feel little social pressure to graduate from high school. With the lure of the street and easy money from the distribution of illegal drugs, they may fail to see the long-term economic returns from education. Mentors, both in- and out-of school, can help overcome these attitudes by making the connection between high school graduation and later success in life.

Although a detailed analysis of the benefits and costs of mentoring students[37] as well as federally funded student mentoring programs[38] are beyond the scope of this work, by continuously supplying individual attention to children, some mentoring programs have achieved remarkable success. For example, Friends of the Children (FoTC), a nonprofit organization founded in 1993, pays trained adults to mentor selected children at least four hours a week from first grade through high school.[39] Mentors visit kindergarten classrooms in distressed neighborhoods to identify those seen by their teachers as likely candidates for incarceration or early pregnancy and follow these youths through high school graduation. The mentors strive to build mentees' social capital, helping them achieve and grow to responsible adults who are ready for postsecondary education or employment. They help mentees work toward grade-level academic performance and provide enriching and challenging experiences based on each child's interests. There are shared activities among mentors so that when a mentor leaves the program, the children are reassigned to another mentor who is familiar with them.

The mentors, who average four to six years in the job, earn salaries comparable to teachers' or social workers' in the local community. Mentors are supported in their challenging work through weekly workshops and educational forums.

Prior to entering the program, each child undergoes up to six weeks of evaluation to determine his or her risk factors (such as poverty and substance abuse in the home) and protective (or capacity) factors (such as IQ and relationship skills) so that he or she can meet the program's intermediate- and long-term goals. The intermediate goals include improved social behavior and emotional control, progress toward positive relationships with adults and peers, no substance abuse, and academic progress. The overall (or long-term) goals are threefold: attaining a high school diploma or GED, no involvement with the juvenile justice system, and no early parenting. To a large measure, the program has achieved these long-term goals.

Based on 2004–2008 data from FoTC-Portland, Oregon affiliate, 85 percent of the mentees earned high school diplomas or GEDs, some 16 percent higher than the national rate. Sixty-eight percent of these children were the first family members to graduate from high school. Although 60 percent of the participants in this FoTC program had at least one incarcerated parent, 95 percent of them stayed out of the juvenile justice system.[40]

The expensive program is labor intensive, with an eight-to-one, mentee to mentor, ratio. It costs about $100,000 per child over the course of twelve years. One study found that the FoTC-Portland, Oregon program's societal benefits that accrue over a lifetime in terms of enhanced educational achievement and lower rates of incarceration, outweighed costs by more than seven to one.[41] Another immediate benefit, avoiding teen pregnancy, helped break the cycle of poverty with 99 percent of the female mentees avoiding teen motherhood, despite 60 percent having been born to a teen parent.[42]

Enhanced Post-High School Earnings

Incorporating career-focused curriculum and work-based learning into high school programs helps students learn relevant workplace skills and enhances their earnings. An analysis of twelve years of longitudinal U.S. data found that students who devoted about one-sixth of their time in high school to occupational-specific vocational courses, that is, they took four advanced CTE courses instead of two academic and one personal interest course, earned at least an extra 12 percent one year after graduating from high school and about 8 percent extra seven years later.[43] The study used the National Educational Longitudinal Study (NELS-88) that followed a nationally representative sample of eighth-grade U.S. students in 1988, every two years through 1994 and then again in 2000. The study focused on high school graduates who were in tenth grade, earned between fifteen and thirty-two Carnegie (academic) units during high school, and graduated in 1992 or 1993. In showing substantial gains in employment and earnings eight years after normal high school graduation, the study held a number of variables constant, including attitudes and abilities in the eighth grade, family background, and college attendance. Computer-related courses had a particularly large impact on earnings eight years posthigh school graduation.

Other studies showed more modest earnings gains for vo-tech students. Seven years after graduation, students earned almost 2 percent (1.9 percent) more for each extra high school occupational course they took; one year or so after graduation they earned 3.2 percent extra.[44] The gains were higher than average for at-risk and minority students.

In sum, offering the students the option of preparing for their chosen occupation during high school improves the labor market outcomes of high school graduates, whether or not they attend and complete higher education. They graduate high school at improved rates and subsequently earned more than those students who did not take CTE courses but do not pursue postsecondary education. A curriculum focused on training students for careers will improve high school graduation rates, especially among black males. These at-risk students find motivation in components, both academic and vocational, with direct links to careers, thereby improving the learning process and overcoming the false dichotomy between knowing and doing. They will also develop sound character traits, such as hard work, self-discipline,[45] and

121

deferred gratification, all of which are important not only to success in high school but also to future achievement. Furthermore, building career-based learning components into the high school curriculum not only complements the academic courses, making them more relevant, but also improves the employment opportunities for those who do not go on to college. Work-based learning, including well-structured work experiences, helps students learn workplace competencies and understand the requirements and operations of specific careers.

Career Academies: A Promising Approach

About 21 percent of all U.S. high schools offer career academies,[46] a small school-within-school approach, that operates within larger schools. Career academies, organized around an occupational or industry focus, weave particular economic sector themes into the curriculum. The academies typically consist of fifty to seventy-five students per grade from the tenth through the twelfth grades. Students take two to four classes a year taught by a common group of teachers, with at least one course being career or occupation-focused, and stay with the same group of teachers from one year to the next.

Aiming to function as "learning communities" of support for students, with the academic and technical curriculum organized around a broad theme, the academies, like CTE programs, attempt to break down the dichotomy between academic and technical subjects. They strive to bring academic rigor to career-related courses and applied learning opportunities to academic courses. The organizational structure partners schools with employers and the local community and also includes work-based learning experiences, such as internships. Through these relationships that connect students to the outside world, local employers support academic programs and sponsor work- and career-related activities for students. These work-based learning programs, developed in collaboration with employer-partners, place students in jobs (or a series of short-term positions) that expose them to various occupations and enable students to gain references for permanent positions.[47]

Career academies offer benefits in terms of earnings gains and improved graduation rates. One study of nine career academies, each of which was the only one in its host high school, demonstrated that the academies induced earnings gains experienced by young males in an experimental group of 1,458 students, 85 percent of whom were black or Hispanic.[48] These young men achieved an 18 percent average gain in earnings, compared with the control group, four years after their scheduled high school graduation. In particular, the earnings gains were concentrated among students with a high or medium risk of dropping out of high school. Also, these impacts persisted for at least eight years after high school graduation. The increase in earnings resulted from helping the young men in the intervention group obtain better-paying jobs and positions that allowed them to work more hours, through full-time, not part-time, jobs. A subsequent follow-up, eight years after scheduled high school graduation, showed that the difference persisted. Among young males, academy students' earnings were 17 percent higher than the control group, or $3,731 per year or nearly $30,000 over the eight years.[49] The eight-year follow-up revealed continued positive impacts on wages and employment rates, with the impacts on hourly wages accounting for nearly one-half of the monthly earnings gains.

This research found that students in career academies did no better or no worse than those in the control group in their standardized academic math and language arts test scores.[50] However, career academies improve high school graduation rates by reducing apathy and alienation, reengaging students, building interest and motivation, and increasing student confidence about their abilities.[51] Although not using matched comparison groups, one study indicated that the high school graduation rates for black California career academy seniors, a self-selected group who may have been more motivated, among other characteristics, during the 2004–2005 year exceeded those of black seniors statewide by 15 percent (96 percent versus 81 percent).[52] Thus, career academies are more likely to retain students than regular high schools, especially those who entered these programs at a high risk of dropping out, thereby providing substantial benefits. As one expert concluded, "Overall, the evidence from career academies points to a highly successful intervention for young men and for students at medium or high risk of dropping out of school."[53]

Educational Policy Recommendations

CTE courses and programs use applied learning that integrates academic and technical subject matter helping students learn in context through a hands-on approach. High school programs leading to promising careers spur student interest in academic courses, thereby improving their academic skills and knowledge. As more students study hard and seek productive careers, a large high school's atmosphere would likely change. Motivated good black students would no longer face antiachievement peer pressure, the burden of "acting white."[54]

Even in the face of declining revenues, school districts need to promote and fund CTE offerings in public high schools. Career academies, in particular, require expansion as do career-themed high schools. However, any good approach can, of course, be undermined by mediocre implementation.

With CTE programs varying widely in terms of type and quality, public sector funders ought to require recipients to track and report student performance, in terms of academic achievement, graduation rates, posthigh school employment, and earnings. Also, moving from a sole reliance on standardized academic tests (and an emphasis on test preparation) to a more comprehensive performance system rests on a broader assessment of student progress and accomplishments, including projects and portfolios, as part of a more well-rounded curriculum that engages students by developing problem-solving and critical thinking.[55] In addition to developing new metrics, evidence-based research must examine what works to improve student outcomes in terms of reducing dropout rates, decreasing high-risk behaviors and alienation, and increasing employment and earnings.

CTE programs must build strong relationships with firms so as to connect students with employers. One study showed the positive impact of employer involvement with individual schools on 1994 labor market outcomes at two years past expected high school graduation.[56] Holding constant various individual community and school characteristics, the study revealed several positive impacts of employer–school partnerships, especially the close linkages between teachers and local firms. The more active the employer–school partnership, the more young people earned, as a result of holding jobs at higher wage rates, and the more likely they avoided unemployment. Employer–school partnerships appeared to raise the share of students graduating on time with a high school diploma, not a GED.

Although local businesses have traditionally played a limited role in shaping CTE courses and programs,[57] they can offer vital input in a variety of areas.[58] Local and state business leaders can help guide curriculum development, course content, and skills lists, thereby linking the needs of the economy to classroom content. Setting up a high school's business and industry advisory committee will bring employers' expertise into vocational education design. It will also build a buy-in among engaged employers, thereby creating more work-based learning opportunities, such as internships and job shadowing, and additional hiring of students educated in a CTE program. Partners in the business community can also provide funding for CTE programs and courses.

More generally, a need exists to align CTE coursework and programs with existing and projected economic conditions and workforce demands, on the local, regional, and state levels. CTE courses and sequences offered must match high-demand/high-growth jobs locally, regionally, and statewide and meet relevant industry standards. In addition, students ought to be trained to be multiskilled, not specialized in a narrow area.

A need also exists to expand the pool of educators qualified to teach rigorous CTE courses and use technology to effectuate cost-efficiencies. Removing unnecessary barriers to credentialing that makes it difficult for those knowledgeable about the workplace and its demands, often midcareer workers and retiring baby boomers, to become CTE teachers, will help expand the pool.[59]

K-12 schools generally can reduce costs by using the power of new technologies. Adopting new technologies that bring superstar teachers to the classroom and using interactive software to facilitate online learning in physical schools offers many benefits, including more efficiently educating children in K-12 system at lower costs, and using the savings to fund higher teacher salaries and more one-on-one tutoring.[60] Permitting outside providers to supplement (or even replace) traditional classroom offerings enables schools to take advantage of their expertise and use these skills to provide services at lower cost than developing the expertise internally.[61] The use of technology and outside providers must, however, take place in the context of personalization in which each student's individual needs are addressed coupled with counseling to guide students facing specific challenges.

Finally, students often hit a wall in middle school, suffering from high rates of teacher burnout coupled with raging hormones and the beginning of the attrition endemic to urban, especially inner city, education.[62] To deal with some of these problems, middle schools could offer programs designed to begin to orient students to the world of work, start to make them aware of career options, and inform them about available high school CTE courses and programs. In developing these career explorations, school districts should provide materials to seventh- and eighth-grade middle school students describing the area's CTE public and charter high school options. These alternatives may inspire students to fulfill their potential and break the one-size-fits-all college prep track mold, recognizing that not everyone benefits from attending college.

Even earlier, beginning in elementary school, a partnership in Cincinnati, Ohio, between the Great Oaks Institute of Technology and Career Development and the local FoTC, discussed earlier, developed an intensive mentoring program using a series of career camps. These camps combined introductions to various career paths with hands-on activities, thereby helping young students see the possibilities of a successful future through CTE.[63]

The Role of Charter Schools

Beyond encouraging public school districts to develop, restore, strengthen, and expand vocational (career and technical) education programs within comprehensive public high schools, special public vo-tech high schools, and regional programs, social entrepreneurs ought to consider opening one or more CTE charter high schools in their locale. Charter schools are publicly financed, that is, tax-funded, but privately run, institutions that exist outside the control of public school boards and generally are not required to adhere to union contracts with their teachers.

Improved Solutions for Urban Systems, Inc. (ISUS) in Dayton, Ohio, provides a charter CTE model.[64] ISUS strives to address the high school dropout problem and better prepare youths for work in high-demand fields. Founded and run by Ann Higdon, ISUS, a nonprofit entity, started in 1992, helps for youths, ages sixteen to twenty-two, many of whom are high school dropouts, earn diplomas and train for jobs. ISUS runs three small, trade-focused charter schools, each with its own facility, in the fields of residential construction, health care, and advanced manufacturing/computer technology. The construction trades program is associated with the local YouthBuild program, a brand name federal program for the disadvantaged, previously discussed in Chapter 2. ISUS students graduate with high school diplomas and can earn college credits while learning and gaining occupational skills in one of these three fields. While the program targets students who have dropped out from traditional high schools, those who are identified as at risk, or are referred from juvenile court or are otherwise troubled, it is designed mainly for reentering young offenders. Total annual student enrollment approaches 400, with 60 percent black, 70 percent male, 75 percent low income, and 80 percent court-involved. Thus, ISUS basically performs a second chance, rehabilitative function, with 87 percent of its graduates employed, in the military, or continuing their education.[65]

At each ISUS charter school, students not only learn in the classroom with small class sizes of twelve to sixteen students and an enviable one to fifteen teacher-to-student ratio, but also obtain hands-on experience at job sites. Its schools operate on a longer school day and year than the local public schools. About one-third of each student's time is spent on academic subjects, one-third on technical training, and one-third on hands-on field work. In addition to using certified teachers, ISUS hires skilled workers from the relevant industries as part-time teachers to fill instructional gaps.

Learning to give back, students engage in community service projects. For example, some build homes for low-income families; others refurbish computers and then donate them to needy youths. In addition to receiving stipends each weekday, they come in on time and ready to work; students obtain industry-recognized credentials.

ISUS also seeks to impart life-changing attitudes and behaviors. It recognizes that its students need more than academic and job skill support. Staffers strive to create a personalized atmosphere with "family meetings" to air student grievances and recognize good deeds.

Some Charter School Considerations for Social Entrepreneurs

Social entrepreneurs contemplating starting a charter school, assuming the existence of enabling legislation, must remember that public sector funds cover some but not all expenses. Generally, these monies can only go to the instructional budget, that is, teacher salaries. Additional funds are needed from federal grants, such as the U.S. Department of Labor YouthBuild program. Contributions from foundations, corporations, and individuals cover other expenses, including getting a charter school up and running, acquiring, rehabilitating, and maintaining the physical space (a school building), purchasing computers and other administrative and instructional equipment, and paying for student transportation.

Similar to public school districts, prospective charter school operators must pay special attention to the occupational field (or fields) a school will offer. It is difficult to forecast where jobs will be four years hence, never mind forty years in the future. Obviously, schools, whether public or charter, should not train for nonexistent jobs or for jobs in fields with no projected employment growth. The U.S. Bureau of Labor Statistics (BLS) biannually forecasts how the nationwide job market will look a decade later and offers employment estimates, including projections of the jobs expected to see the largest numerical and percentage growth during the next decade.[66] Regional and local employment projections must also be consulted to zero in on fields that only require vocational high school or on-the-job training (or both). Possibilities include technicians who install, repair, and debug computers and high-tech instruments in various fields such as health care, transportation, and distribution, as well as jobs that are hard to automate, such as home- and nursing-home-based elder care, hospitality, carpentry, digital graphics, HVAC, masonry, plumbing, and auto repair. Construction, which will come back, but not in the near-term, offers high-paying jobs for people who are good at what they do. Mechanics and repair specialists should also continue to be in demand.

Whether a CTE program takes the form of a charter high school or is part of public high school program, building a sound employer–school partnership is essential. Programs must engage and partner with businesses.

A Non-Vo-tech High School Alternative

Job-training alternatives exist apart from brick-and-mortar vo-tech high schools. For example, The Excel Institute's Automotive Workforce Development Training Program, based in Washington, DC, provides vocational training in automotive technology for at-risk youths and adults.[67]

Founded in 1997 by George Starke, a former professional football player, and John W. Lyon, the CEO of a parking management company, Excel, a nonprofit entity, accepts a diverse, open enrollment student body. Its students include multiple age groups, various ethnicities, men and women, individuals with a history of crime (some 15 percent of its students are directly referred by the court system) or substance abuse, high school dropouts, the unemployed and underemployed, above the age of sixteen from the Washington, DC, area who want to build a better life for themselves in the high-demand, high-paying automotive technology field. Serving both preventive and rehabilitative functions, it strives to introduce students to a new peer group, so they will spend less time surrounded by those with few links to the gainful, legal employment, where learning is often denigrated. The one-year program typically graduates some forty students each year, for example, forty-two in 2009 and thirty-eight in 2011. About half of its 2011 graduates had jobs on graduation, with a starting wage of ten to twenty-five dollars per hour, depending on specialty, plus benefits.

In the Excel program, students, who do not possess a high school diploma or GED and/or are assessed below tenth-grade reading and/or math level, about 30 percent of its current student population, begin with a comprehensive approach in phase one that includes GED instruction, basic literacy skills (applied language, math, and science) as well as life skills and employability training. Its Applied Language Arts class helps students organize and express applied technical information in oral and written formats. Excel's Applied Math and Science courses focus on mathematics and science skills used in the automotive service field.

In the next phase, Excel's automotive curriculum focuses on a competency-based learning process designed to develop student skills and knowledge in becoming automotive service technicians. The curriculum identifies and prioritizes required competencies in various specialties: brake systems (principles of operation and types, diagnosis, services, and repair of brake systems), basic electronics (theory and application including mechanical assemblies, electrical circuitry, and basic understanding of electrical concepts and how common electrical components work), automotive electrical/electronic systems (automotive electrical theory and hands-on application of wiring/repair/replacement of batteries, starters, alternators, electrical accessories, and electrical/electronic components), and steering and suspension systems (diagnosis, service, and repair of automotive steering and suspension systems). The program also includes an introduction to automotive technology (identifying tools and equipment associated with auto repair, obtaining critical repair information and specifications, raising vehicles on lifts and jacks, identifying and checking major vehicle fluids, systems, and components, including engine oil and filter change, chassis and suspension lubrication, measuring tire pressure and tread depth, dismounting, mounting, and balancing tires, replacing wiper blades, bulbs, and testing and servicing batteries) and safety and pollution prevention as well as two optional electives, engine repair and heating and air conditioning.

The competency-based training takes into account each student's knowledge and attitudes. It requires student performance as the main evidence of achievement. The Excel training model allows students a more individualized, self-paced method of progressing through this part of the program. Training in the automotive curriculum includes hands-on, textbook, and on-line instruction. Students recognize the connection of the instructional efforts to success in their future careers.

Competency-based certificates play an important role in Excel's program. The National Automotive Technical Education Foundation has approved Excel's technical curriculum. Excel also provides students with an Automotive Service Excellence Certificate on completion of the program. The competency certificate offers convincing evidence to potential employees that the recipients are worth hiring.

Excel offers a brief workforce development course to prepare students to compete for employment. Topics include resume and cover letter preparation, developing an interview strategy and techniques, applying for job positions, and performing follow-through procedures.

In addition to phase one, the technical curriculum, and the workforce development course, in Excel's Life and Employability Skills Training part of the program, provided in partnership with the Family Health and Education Institute, Inc., students receive comprehensive social and educational services designed to increase their academic attainment, improve their mental and emotional well-being, and enhance their marketable job skills. Thus, as exemplified by Excel, an organization can offer technical training in a much more modest facility and partner with other entities offering education, such as GED preparation and various social services and supports.

Individuals trained in CTE and alternative programs come into the labor market with a skill set and some type of work record. No longer will they be confined to the margins of the economy and society for the rest of their lives. Also CTE and alternative programs could expand their reach by providing entrepreneurial training,[68] thereby offering a path to self-employment for those desiring this route.

CTE and alternative programs will help renew hope among those who otherwise would harm themselves and others through crime, drugs, or nonmarital, teen pregnancies. By facilitating economic self-sufficiency, these programs will help bring the urban underclass into the nation's mainstream economic and social life, thereby providing benefits for the participants and society as a whole.

Notes

1. Peter Goldschmidt and Jia Wang, "When Can Schools Affect Dropout Behavior? A Longitudinal Multilevel Analysis," *American Educational Research Journal* 36, no. 4 (Winter 1999): 715–38, at 716; Zeng-yin Chen and Howard B. Kaplan, "Social Failure in Early Adolescence and Status Attainment in Middle Adulthood: A Longitudinal Study," *Sociology of Education* 76, no. 2 (April 2003): 110–27; Jennifer Laird, "Dropout and Completion Rates in the United States: 2006," Compendium Report, U.S. Department of Education, National Center for Education Statistics, NCES 2008-053, September 2008, 1.

2. Henry M. Levin and others, "The Public Returns to Public Educational Investments in African-American Males," *Economics of Education Review* 26 (2007): 700–9, at 704–5. See also Henry M. Levin and Cecilia E. Rouse, "The True Cost of High School Dropouts," *New York Times*, January 26, 2012, A23.

3. The statistics in this paragraph are from Lance Lochner and Enrico Moretti, "The Effect of Education on Crime: Evidence from Prison Inmates, Arrest, and Self-Reports," *American Economic Review* 94, no. 1 (March 2004): 155–89, at 160 (Table 2 Census Incarceration Rates for Men by Education [In Percentage Terms]), 181 (Table 13 Social Costs per Crime and Social Benefits of Increasing High School Completion Rate by 1 Percent). See also Levin and others, "The Public Returns," 706.

4. Public Law 347. The Balanced Budget Act of 1997 (Public Law 105-33) repealed the Smith-Hughes Act.

5. Public Law 88-210.

6. The National Commission on Excellence in Education, *A Nation at Risk: The Imperative for Educational Reform*, April 1983.

7. Public Law 98-524.

8. The Carl D. Perkins Vocational and Technical Education Act of 1998, Public Law 105-332. See also Rebecca R. Skinner and Richard N. Apling, "The Carl D. Perkins Vocational and Technical Education Act of 1998: Background and Implementation," Congressional Research Service, May 10, 2005, RL31747.

9. Public Law 109-270. For a detailed analysis of the 2006 Perkins Act see John M. Laughner, "The Carl Perkins Career and Technical Education Improvement Act of 2006 (Analysis)," FBA Inc., November 15, 2006. See also Association for Career and Technical Education, "Summary and Analysis of Major Provisions and Changes Career and Technical Education Improvement Act of 2006," August 4, 2006. The Obama administration proposed a 20 percent reduction in its fiscal 2012 budget for career and technical education to a little more than $1 billion. Office of Management and Budget, "Fiscal Year 2012 Budget of the U.S. Government," Appendix, 353 (Office of Vocational and Adult Education). See also Motoko Rich, "Tough Budget Calculus as Technical Schools Face Deep Cuts," *New York Times*, July 10, 2011, 1.

10. John L. Scott and Michelle Sarkees-Wircenski, *Overview of Career and Technical Education*, 4th ed. (Homewood, IL: American Technical Publishers, 2008), 311. See also Peter Edelman and others, *Reconnecting Disadvantaged Young Men* (Washington, DC: Urban Institute, 2006), 46.

11. John H. Bishop and Ferran Mane, "The Impacts of Career-Technical Education on High School Labor Market Success," *Economics of Education Review* 23, no. 4 (August 2004): 381–402, at 397.

12. For an overview of guidance counseling and job placement see Marie Cohen and Douglas J. Besharov, "The Important Role of Career and Technical Education: Implications for Federal Policy," revised May 2004, 31–33. For background on high school guidance counselors and their influence on students and their parents see James E. Rosenbaum, *Beyond College for All: Career Paths for the Forgotten Half* (New York: Russell Sage, 2001), 88–107.

13. The statistics are from Ethan Yazzie-Mintz, "Charting the Path from Engagement to Achievement: A Report on the 2009 High School Survey of Student Engagement (HSSSE)," Center for Evaluation & Education, Indiana University, School of Education, 6. These responses regarding boredom were consistent during the four years (2006–2009) of HSSSE survey administrations. Ibid., 7.

14. Robert Weissberg, *Bad Students, Not Bad Schools* (New Brunswick, NJ: Transaction, 2010), 23–28, 35–39.

15. See generally, Howard Gardner, *Frames of Mind: The Theory Multiple Intelligences* (New York: Basic, 1983). See also Daniel Goleman, *Emotional Intelligence* (New York: Bantam, 1995).

16. See, e.g., Catherine Rampell, "Many with New College Degree Find the Job Market Humbling," *New York Times*, May 19, 2011, A1. But see David Leonhardt, "Even for Cashiers, College Pays Off," *New York Times*, June 26, 2011, Week in Review Section, 3.

17. For jobs that do not require a college degree but pay above the national average for those who processes the requisite skills see Harry J. Holzer and Robert I. Lerman, "America's Forgotten Middle-Skill Jobs: Education And Training Requirements in the Next Decade and Beyond, Skills2Compete Campaign," Workforce Alliance, November 2007. See also William McGurn, "Labor Day and the American Dream," *Wall Street Journal*, September 1, 2009, A15; John Ratzenberger, "Help Wanted: Skilled Workers Need Apply," *Investor's Business Daily*, June 30, 2010, A11; Carol Morello, "Tossing the Grades, Jumping into the Trades," *Washington Post*, June 15, 2010, B1; James R. Hagerty, "Help Wanted on Factory Floor," *Wall Street Journal*, May 6, 2011, A1.

18. Matthew B. Crawford, *Shop Class as Soulcraft: An Inquiry into the Value of Work* (New York: Penguin, 2009), who turned from the head of a DC think tank to open a motorcycle repair shop. See also Matthew B. Crawford, "The Case for Working with Your Hands," *New York Times Magazine*, May 24, 2009, 34–41; Sarah Kershaw, "Deskbound, Romancing the Brick," *New York Times*, August 27, 2009, E1.

19. Charles Murray, *Real Education: Four Simple Truths for Bringing America's Schools Back to Reality* (New York: Crown Forum, 2008), 147–50, 168; Charles Murray, "What's Wrong with Vocational School," *Wall Street Journal*, January 17, 2007, A19. See generally, Rosenbaum, *Beyond College for All*.

20. National Commission on Excellence in Education, *A Nation at Risk*.

21. See generally, Robert I. Lerman, "Career-Focused Education and Training for Youth," in *Reshaping the American Workforce in a Changing Economy*, ed. Harry J. Holzer and Demetra Smith Nightingale (Washington, DC: Urban Institute, 2007), 51–52; Bishop and Mane, "Impact of Career-Technical Education," 382.

22. Marcia Silverberg and others, *National Assessment of Vocational Education: Final Report to Congress*, U.S. Department of Education, 2004, xxi, xxv, 18–19, 26, 30, 93–95; Karen Levesque and others, "Career and Technical Education in the United States: 1990 to 2005," U.S. Department of Education, National Center for Education Statistics, NCES 2008-035, July 2005, 44, 73, 221. See also Cohen and Besharov, "Important Role," 19–22.

23. Lerman, "Career-Focused Education," 55; Bishop and Mane, "Impacts of Career-Technical Education," 381–82.

24. Levesque and others, "Career and Technical Education," 8, 15, 17; Cohen and Besharov, "Important Role," 22–26, provided an overview of current CTE programs.

25. Levesque and others, "Career and Technical Education," 15, 71, 218.

26. Lisa Hudson and Jennifer Laird, "New Indicators of High School Career/Technical Education Coursetaking: Class of 2005," National Center for Education Statistics, NCES 2009-038, April 2007.

27. Levesque and others, "Career and Technical Education," 26, 71, 218.

28. Ibid., 8, 217.

29. Ibid., 13.

30. Silverberg and others, *National Assessment*, 102–3. Drawing on a sample of students who attended high school during the late 1980s to the early 1990s, Roberto Agodini and John Deke, "The Relationship between High School Vocational Education and Dropping out," Mathematica Policy Research, MPR No. 8879-400, February 2004, found no difference in the average high school's students chance of dropping out whether following the vocational concentrator or the basic academic program.

31. Bishop and Mane, "Impacts of Career-Technical Education," 385–86.

32. Stephen B. Plank and others, "High School Dropout and the Role of Career and Technical Education: A Survival Analysis of Surviving High School," *Sociology of Education* 81, no. 4 (October 2008): 345–70; Stephen B. Plank, "A Question of Balance: CTE, Academic Courses, High School Persistence, and Student Achievement," *Journal of Vocational Education* 26, no. 3 (2001): 279–327, placed the ideal mix at three CTE credits to four academic credits.

33. James Kulik, "Curricular Tracks and High School Vocational Education," in *The Quality of Vocational Education: Background Papers from the 1994 National Assessment of Vocational Education* (U.S. Department of Education, Office of Educational Research and Improvement, June 1998), 82–93, at 93. See also Kenneth A. Rasinski and Steven Pedlow, "Using Transcripts to Study the Effectiveness of Vocational Education," *Journal of Vocational Education Research* 19, no. 3 (1994): 23–43, at 29–36, 39–40. Cohen and Besharov, "Important Role," 42–43, summarized the findings on dropout rates. They also evaluated the research on the educational attainment of vocational students. Ibid., 44. One study of twenty-seven regional

vocational–technical education high schools in Massachusetts found that these students vastly improved their passing rates on English and math-standardized tests between 2001 and 2007, a period marked by schools focusing on integrating academic instruction into technical classes. By 2007, the vocational students passed these tests at higher rates than other students in state. Alison L. Fraser, "Vocational-Technical Education in Massachusetts," A Pioneer Institute White Paper, No. 42, October 2008, 5–7. For a critical assessment of the impact of CTE high schools on academic achievement see Kristy Bailey, "N.C.'s Technical High Schools Graduate, But do They Education?" *Carolina Journal*, February 2011, 7.

34.   Peter D. Hart Research Associates, Inc., "Report Findings Based on a Survey among California Ninth and Tenth Graders," April 5, 2006. See also Catherine Gewertz, "H.S. Dropouts Say Lack of Motivation Top Reason to Quit," *Education Week* 25, no. 26 (March 8, 2008): 1. For a comprehensive analysis see Russell W. Rumberger, "Why Students Drop Out of School," in *Dropouts in America: Confronting the Graduation Rate Crisis*, ed. Gary Orfield (Cambridge, MA: Harvard Education, 2004), 131–55. The general conditions needed for student motivation and assessment include small class size, environments where students play a greater role in their own learnings, a clearly structured, coherent curriculum, and relevance to the outside world. See National Research Council, *Engaging Schools: Fostering High School Students' Motivation to Learn* (Washington, DC: National Academies, 2004), 31–55.

35.   Levesque and others, "Career and Technical Education," 23.

36.   John M. Bridgeland and others, "The Silent Epidemic: Perspectives of High School Dropouts," Civic Enterprises, March 2006, 13.

37.   Research on the effectiveness of work-based mentoring in terms of skills enhancement, social networking, and enhanced self-concept was summarized in Jean Rhodes, "Research Corner; Work based Mentoring," July 2003, 2–4. See also, Thomas J. Smith, "Guides for the Journey: Supporting High-Risk Youth with Paid Mentors and Counselors," Public/Private Ventures, P/PV Briefs, June 2004.

Big Brothers Big Sisters (BBBS) serves as the exemplar of a mentoring program. Joseph P. Tierney and Jean Baldwin Grossman with Nancy L. Resch, "Making a Difference: An Impact Study of Big Brothers Big Sisters," Public/Private Ventures, September 2000, iii, 20, 22, concluded that the program had some beneficial impacts, such as decreasing the onset of illegal drug use. See also Linda Jucovy and Carla Herrera, "High School Mentors in Brief: Findings from the Big Brothers Big Sisters School-Based Mentoring Impact Study," Public/Private Ventures, P/PV in Brief 8, October 2010; David L. DuBois and others, "Testing a New Model of Mentoring," *A Critical View of Youth Mentoring: New Directions for Youth Development* 93 (Spring 2002): 21–57, at 46–47; Jean Baldwin Grossman and Joseph P. Tierney, "Does Mentoring Work? An Impact Study of the Big Brothers Big Sisters Program," *Evaluation Review* 22, no. 3 (June 1998): 403–26, at 41316, found that large randomized evaluation of BBBS's school-based mentoring program produced mixed results. At the end of the school year, the mentored youth showed small, but significant, improvements in academic performance and attendance compared to the nonmentored control group. In a reassessment a few months into the following school year, the significant findings generally eroded to nonsignificance. Carla Herrera and others, "Making a Difference in Schools: The Big Brothers Big Sisters School-Based Mentoring Impact Study," Public/Private Ventures, 2007, 51–52.

For a cost-benefit summary of youth mentoring research see Brian T. Yates, "Cost-Benefit and Cost-Effectiveness," in *Handbook of Youth Mentoring*, ed. DuBois and Karcher (Thousand Oaks, CA: Sage, 2005), 525–45, who concluded that reliable data on cost-benefit ratios and cost-effectiveness for mentoring programs was not then available; Steve Aos and others, "Benefits and Costs of Preventive and Early Intervention Programs for Youth," Washington State Institute for Public Policy, September 17, 2004, 6 (Table 1 Summary of Benefits and Costs [2003 Dollars] of mentoring programs in the Washington State juvenile justice system); Douglas L. Fountain and Amy Arbreton, "The Cost of Mentoring," in *Contemporary Issues in Mentoring*, ed. Jean Baldwin Grossman (Philadelphia, PA: Public/Private Ventures, 1998), 48–65.

For a methodology overview see Jean Baldwin Grossman, "Evaluating Mentoring Programs," Public/Private Ventures, P/PV Brief, September 2009.

38.   For a summary of three federal mentoring programs, Mentoring Children of Prisoners Program (Department of Health and Human Services), Safe and Drug Free Schools Mentoring Program (Department of Education), and Mentoring Initiative for System-Involved Youth (Department of Justice) see Adrienne L. Fernandes, "Vulnerable Youth: Federal Mentoring Programs and Issues," Congressional Research Service, updated June 20, 2008, Report RL34306. Evaluations of federally funded mentoring programs include Lawrence Bernstein and others, "Impact Evaluation of the U.S. Department of Education's Student Mentoring Program," Final Report, March 2009, U.S. Department of Education, National Center for Education Evaluation and Regional Assistance, Institute of Education Sciences, NCEE 2009-4047; U.S. General Accounting Office, "Student Mentoring Programs: Education's Monitoring and Information Sharing could be Improved," June 2004, GAO-04-581.

39.   Friends of the Children (FoTC), "About Us" (About Friends of the Children, Children are identified for our program in kindergarten with risk factors), http://www.friendschildren.org/about-us (accessed May 25, 2011); FoTC-Portland, "Who is a Friend," http://www.friendschldren. org/portland/friend.html (accessed May 25, 2011); "History," http://www. friendschldren.org/portland/history.html (accessed May 25, 2011). See also David L. Kirp, "The Kids are All Right," *Nation* 292, no. 9 (February 28, 2011): 22–26; Irene Wielawski, "Mentoring Young People," in *To Improve Health and Health Care: The Robert Wood Johnson Foundation Anthology*, vol. 11 (San Francisco, CA: Jossey-Bass 2008), 183–88.

40.   FoTC, "Measures of Success," http://www.friendschildren.org/friends-works/meansure-of-success (accessed May 25, 2011); FoTC-Portland, "About Us," http://www.friendschildren.org/portland/aboutus.html (accessed May 25, 2011). See also David L. Kirp, "The Wildest Achievement Gap," *National Affairs* 5 (Fall 2010): 54–74, at 72–73; Interview with Duncan

Campbell, "Mentoring the Least of These," *Reclaiming Children and Youth* 14, no. 2 (Summer 2005): 91–92.

41. Benefitics LLC, "Return on Investment: Friends of the Children Portland," Fact Sheet, 2011.

42. FoTC-Portland, "About Us."

43. Bishop and Mane, "Impacts of Career-Technical Education," 389–91. See also Ferran Mane, "Trends in the Payoff to Academic and Occupation-Specific Skills: The Short and Medium Run Returns to Academic and Vocational High School Courses for Non-College-Bound Students," *Economics of Education Review* 18, no. 4 (October 1999): 417–37; Cohen and Besharov, "Important Role," 45, summarized the studies reporting labor market gains from vocational education.

44. Silverberg and others, *National Assessment*, xix, 18, 111–12. Another report found no systematic relationship between the occupational credits that male graduates from the class of 1992 earned in high school and their full-time earnings in 1999. The more occupational credits that these male graduates earned in high school, the higher their part-time earnings in 1999 in comparison to their male classmates who took no occupational coursework in high school. Levesque and others, "Career and Technical Education," 68, 73–74.

45. One study of 140 eighth-grade students found that self-discipline accounted for more than twice as much variance as IQ in final grades, school attendance, and hours spent doing homework. Angela L. Duckworth and Martin E. P. Seligman, "Self-Discipline Outdoes IQ in Predicting Academic Performance of Adolescents," *Psychological Science* 16, no. 12 (December 2005): 939–44. See also Jonah Lehrer, "Learning How to Focus on Focus," *Wall Street Journal*, September 3–4, 2011, C12; Tara Parker-Pope, "School Curriculum Falls Short on Bigger Lessons," *New York Times*, September 6, 2011, D5.

46. James Kemple with Judith Scott-Clayton, "Career Academies: Impacts on Labor Market Outcomes and Educational Attainment," MDRC, March 2004, 3; Levesque, "Career and Technical Education," 23, 25 (Table 2.15 Percentage and number of public schools with a 12th grade that offered career academies, by selected school characteristics: 2004). For background on theme-based learning communities see National Research Council, *Engaging Schools*, 168–86; David Stern and others, "Career Academics: Building Blocks for Reconstructing American High Schools," Career Academy Support Network, Graduate School of Education, University of California at Berkeley, October 2001. For a description of the origins of career academy programs and early evaluation results see David Stern and others, *Career Academies: Partnerships for Reconstructing American High Schools* (San Francisco, CA: Jossey-Bass, 1992); David Stern and others, "Career Academies: A Proven Strategy to Prepare High School Students for College and Careers," Career Academy Support Network, Graduate School of Education, University of California, Berkeley, 2010, 2–4, 6–7, provided an overview of the origins, growth, and evolution of career academies. For examples of successful career academies see Patricia Clark and others, "Can Combining Academic and Career-Technical Education Improve High School Outcomes in

California?" California Dropout Research Project Report #4, Gevitz Graduate School of Education, University of California, Santa Barbara, October 2007, 32–69.

47. I have drawn on Kemple with Scott-Clayton, "Career Academies," 3–4. See also Lerman, "Career-Focused Education," 61–62.

48. Kemple with Scott-Clayton, "Career Academies," ES-3 to ES-5, 10–22, 39.

49. James J. Kemple with Cynthia J. Willner, "Career Academies: Long-Term Impacts on Labor Market Outcomes, Educational Attainment, and Transitions to Adulthood," MDRC, June 2008, iii, 16–20.

50. Kemple with Scott-Clayton, "Career Academies," ES-5 to ES-7, 22–25. See also Silverberg and others, *National Assessment*, 100.

51. James J. Kemple and Jason C. Snipes, "Career Academies: Impacts on Students' Engagement and Performance in High School," MDRC, March 2000, 43–73, concluded that career academies had retained a larger portion of the high-risk students whose initial characteristics made them more likely to drop out of high school. See also Lerman, "Career-Focused Education," 53–54, 61–62.

52. ConnectEd: The California Center for College and Career and The Career Academy Support Network, University of California Berkeley, "A Profile of the California Partnership Academies 2004-2005," March 2007, 18, 19 (Figure 16 CPA and California 12th-Grade Graduation Rates By Race/Ethnicity).

53. Lerman, "Career-Focused Education," 62.

54. Signithia Fordham and John U. Ogbu developed an oppositional culture theory as the basis for black students' underachievement in "Black Students' School Success: Coping with the 'Burden of Acting White,'" *Urban Review* 18, no. 3 (September 1986): 176–206. For an analysis of the impact of social pressures see Roland G. Fryer, "Acting White," *Education Next* 6, no. 1 (Winter 2006): 53–59. See also David Austen-Smith and Roland G. Fryer, Jr., "An Economic Analysis of 'Acting White.'"

55. See, e.g., Fernanda Santos, "A Trial Run for School Standards that Encourage Deeper Thought," *New York Times*, April 25, 2011, A1.

56. John Bishop and Ferran Mane, "The Impacts of School-Business Partnerships on the Early Labor Market Success of Students," in *The School-to-Work Movement: Origins and Destinations*, ed. William Stull and Nicholas Sanders (Westport, CT: Praeger, 2003), 195, 200.

57. Silverberg and others, "National Assessment," 72–73.

58. For an overview of strategies to facilitate employer and higher education support see Charles Dayton with Susan Tidyman, "Partnership Guide for Career Academies," Careers Academy Support Network, Graduate School of Education, University of California, Berkeley, 2010, 7–10, 12–27.

59. State of California, Little Hoover Commission, "Career Technical Education: Creating Options for High School Success," November 2007, vi–vii, 41–47.

60. Clayton M. Christensen and others, *Disrupting Class: How Disruptive Innovation will Change the Way the World Learns* (New York: McGraw Hill, 2008), 21–42, 89–145; Terry M. Moe and John E. Chub, *Liberating Learning: Technology, Politics, and the Future of American Education* (San Francisco,

CA: Jossey-Bass, 2009), 1–12, 57–98. See also Sam Dillon, "Foundations Join to Offer Online Courses for Schools," *New York Times*, April 28, 2011, A18; Trip Gabriel, "More Pupils are Learning Online, Fueling Debate on Quality," *New York Times*, April 6, 2011, A1; Matt Richtel, "In Classrooms of Future, Stagnant Scores," *New York Times*, September 4, 2011, A1.

61. Frederick M. Hess and Olivia Meeks, "From School Choice to Educational Choice," American Enterprise Institute for Public Policy Research, Education Outlook No. 3, April 2011, 4.

62. On the transition from middle school to high school see Jean Baldwin Grossman and Siobhan M. Cooney, "Paving the Way for Success in High School and Beyond: The Importance of Preparing Middle School Students for the Transition to Ninth Grade," Public/Private Ventures, January 2009.

63. Ann Jordan, "Career Exploration for At-Risk Students," *Techniques* 81, no. 3 (March 2006): 20–21.

64. Interview by author of Ann Higdon, June 1, 2010. See also Kristi Essick, "To Believe in Someone," *Wall Street Journal*, May 15–16, 2010, R5; Jennie Szink, "Construction Company, School Build Partnership," *Dayton Daily News* (OH), July 19, 2009, C1; Scott Elliott, "Labor Secretary Visits ISUS in Dayton," *Dayton Daily News* (OH), October 13, 2007, A4; Sean Strader, "Building Character," *Dayton Daily News* (OH), July 15, 2005, B1; Nancy Martin and Samuel Halperin, "Whatever it Takes: How Twelve Communities are Reconnecting Out-of-School Youth," American Youth Policy Forum, 2006, 14–17.

65. Martin and Halperin, "Whatever it Takes," 16.

66. See, e.g., T. Alan Lacey and Benjamin Wright, "Occupational Employment Projections to 2018," *Monthly Labor Review* 132, no. 11 (November 2009): 82–123.

67. Interview by author of Cheryl Edwards, September 15, 2011; email to author from Cheryl Edwards, September 15, 2011; Excel Institute (Excel), "About the Excel Institute," http://www.theexcelinstitute.org/index.php. (accessed May 16, 2011); "Course Descriptions," http://www.theexcelinstitute.or/index.php (accessed May 16, 2011); "Excel 2009 Annual Report," 2–3, 8–11; "Excel Annual Report 2010," 2–3, 8–9. See also Cheryl W. Thompson, "A Jump-Start for a Productive Life," *Washington Post*, April 22, 1999, J1.

68. The Network for Teaching Entrepreneurship (NFTE) works with teachers in high schools located low-income communities to introduce students to entrepreneurship and open their possibilities for the future. NFTE offers a sixty-five-hour semester or year-long classroom program, culminating in the preparation of a business plan, and Biz Camps, a one- or two-week day camp for teens interested in entrepreneurship. Network for Teaching Entrepreneurship, "Mission & History," http://www.nfte.com/what/mission) (accessed May 25, 2011); "Classroom Programs," http://www.nfte.com/what/classroom-programs (accessed May 25, 2011); "BizCamps," http://www.nfte.com/what/bizcamps (accessed May 25, 2011). In 2011, NITE launched Start Up Summer, a new program for students who wanted to launch their business ideas and gain experience from executing a business plan. NFTE, "Advanced Programs," http://www.nfte.com/print/what/advanced-programs (accessed May 25, 2011); Aspen Youth

Entrepreneurship Strategies Group, "Youth Entrepreneurship Education in America: A Policymaker's Action Guide," Aspen Institute, 2008, 19, 21–22, urged local policymakers to introduce entrepreneurship training in all schools, especially those with large population of youth from low-income communities. See also Barbara Haislip, "How to Raise an Entrepreneur," *Wall Street Journal*, June 13, 2011, R3.

5

Conclusion: The Need to Rethink Three Policies

Devising policies, programs, and strategies so that generations of children will no longer grow up where they lack a fair chance of becoming the adults they might be represents a challenge. The approaches advocated in this book will hopefully provide people with opportunities to make the most of their human capital, the individual resources, such as abilities, education, and job skills, each of us brings to the economic marketplace (and thus collectively make the most of America's human capital), provided they act responsibly. I believe that each of us should have the opportunity to fulfill his or her potential, achieving a life with dignity, a life with meaning. It is, however, difficult to formulate policies, programs, and strategies to deal with the fact that some people get the short straw in life on various dimensions they lack control over, but not waste funds and possibly generate unintended, negative consequences that may be worse than the original difficulties.

This book advocates two approaches designed to help inner city blacks, particularly males, fulfill their potential. In the near-term, nonprofit organizations, funded by increased donations from foundations, wealthy individuals, and corporations, could provide enhanced, empirically verifiable rehabilitative efforts, including job and entrepreneurial training, transitional jobs, and transportation, together with a comprehensive array of social services. Looking to the intermediate-term, a new emphasis on skills training through vocational (career and technical) education in America's urban high schools as well as alternative venues offers a promising approach. A focus on building character, including self-discipline, perseverance, and the ability to defer gratification, underpins and defines both of these strategies. Hopefully more members of the inner city black underclass will be able to enter and stay in the middle class through earning legitimate

141

livelihoods. The public sector will collect more in taxes from those gainfully employed and devote less public funds to welfare and the criminal justice system.

I realize today that it is hard to get ahead and join the American mainstream, especially for disconnected youths and adults, and exponentially more difficult for ex-offenders, but "one's efforts can and often will succeed."[1] By improving the quality of America's workforce through building human capital at the socioeconomic bottom and unlocking the potential of inner city blacks, we can, however, make a start to providing hope and enabling more people to fend for themselves, thereby weaning them from dependency on public sector handouts.

To facilitate these efforts in an era of public sector austerity, I would offer three further suggestions focused on rethinking: first, the barriers to gaining employment and occupational licensing and obtaining a driver's license encountered by ex-offenders; second, childrearing patterns and toxic neighborhoods, and third, the War on Drugs.

Rethinking the Barriers to Employment and Occupational Licensing

Policymakers need to review federal and state laws that limit the employment or licensing of those with criminal convictions. Balancing the protection of the public against the desire to reintegrate former prisoners into society, they ought to reconsider the public safety objectives of these barriers. Unintended consequences may result from these restrictions, for example, the ability of nonviolent ex-felons to become barbers. Specifically, those denied a livelihood may turn to criminal activities. Reconsideration may lead to narrowing the range of crimes subject to these barriers, excluding only those individuals who represent a social danger, or limiting the timeframe during which these restrictions apply postincarceration.

The revocation or suspension of drivers' licenses for those convicted of drug offenses also requires reevaluation. Policymakers ought to rethink the federal mandate imposed on states to revoke or suspend a driver's license as a result of a nondriving-related drug conviction. Apart from repeal, possibilities include limiting the revocation or suspension to driving-related drug offenses or offering limited licenses so impacted individuals can at least get to work and receive drug treatment and other health services.

Rethinking Childrearing Patterns and
Toxic Neighborhoods

Family poverty and dysfunctionality in combination with toxic neighborhoods represent huge disadvantages for any child to overcome. Today's best programs, such as the Harlem Children's Zone, link a comprehensive menu of social services with K-12 charter schools. These programs for underclass children offer an alternative to an often nonexistent, disorganized family life, set in the context of mean streets, predatory gangs, and drug-infested neighborhoods. They seek to improve the lives of children through a continuous series of integrated interventions until they graduate not only from high school but also from college.

Black inner city children from chaotic single-parent homes need to enter adolescence, as most middle class children do, with sound, internalized models in their heads—controlling their impulses, working hard, planning for the future, and developing self-discipline and the self-motivational skills needed for success. Achieving these goals likely requires the implementation of intrusive programs.

The libertarian in me—allowing parents to raise their children as they see fit—rebels at suggesting an approach that smacks of the Nanny State. Yet, this type of approach may be needed.

It may be necessary to go far beyond a "nudge"[2] to help inner city parents and children make rational choices that they otherwise would not make. Under a nudge approach, by carefully placing choices, for example, children in a school cafeteria can be guided to select fruit for dessert, rather than marshmallows. In other words, in a nudge state the government gives citizens the freedom to make their own choices, but arranges the choices in ways designed to overcome their irrationality or lethargy for their own good or the common good.

However, thorny societal problems, from the home environment to the toxic neighborhood, may require much more than a nudge. It may require a shove to give children the stable, nurturing structure they otherwise would lack at home. We may need rather invasive interventions that participants enter into voluntarily to alter childrearing practices and teach virtues and behaviors, truly the Nanny State, what I call Synthetic Families, to development human capital. Otherwise, generation after generation of children who do not come from intact, organized families and nontoxic neighborhoods will fall further behind their peers in the global knowledge economy.

Federal efforts to facilitate healthy marriages and two-parent families, reduce nonmarital childbearing and promote responsible fatherhood, particularly the 1996 Personal Responsibility and Work Opportunity Reconciliation Act[3] and its 2006 reauthorization,[4] have failed to achieve the desired results. Over the past decade and a half, nonmarital childbearing among blacks has not decreased; black males have not become more responsible fathers. It is difficult to develop two-parent biological families among African-Americans. Researchers found that low-income black females value, even prize, marriage, but they do not see many marriageable partners in their midst, in part, because there are not that many employed black males, who are free from the grasp of the criminal justice system.[5] They held marriage in such high esteem that they were reluctant to marry until they and their potential mates were emotionally and financially prepared to do so. Many had little confidence that their cohabiting partners would ever become marriage material. Thus, waiting until marriage to bear children would place them at high risk of never becoming mothers.

Efforts to encourage black, unmarried fathers to take more responsibility for their children have also faltered. Along with President Barack Obama's exhortation[6] to change fathers' attitudes and behaviors, federal efforts have focused on enhanced child support enforcement. According to one study, blacks take a different, non-monetary view of fatherhood, emphasizing the importance of a good father being emotionally involved, spending time with his children, providing paternal guidance and role modeling, and doing caregiving tasks.[7] African-Americans typically view the formal, mandatory child support system as unnecessarily invasive and potentially weakening a father's commitment to his children. In short, policymakers have encountered difficulties in making black males assume their roles as fathers and providers.

To compensate for nonmarital childbearing, often dysfunctional single-mother family units, and absence of biological fathers, policymakers may turn to synthetic family structures. This approach begins with home visit interventions in childrearing, pioneered by the Nurse–Family Partnership, and the comprehensive approach of the Harlem Children's Zone.

Changing Childrearing Practices: Nurse–Family Partnership

Attentive, careful parenting serves as a first step to overcoming the culture of poverty, even in toxic neighborhoods. Parenting programs help surmount the disparities in how poverty-stricken single mothers, if left alone, often shape their children's future by stunting their verbal abilities and teaching the norms of resignation, as discussed in Chapter 1.

Home visit programs, such as the Nurse–Family Partnership, which began in 1977,[8] use trained nurses and other professionals to provide support and guidance to young, low-income, first-time mothers before the end of the second trimester of pregnancy through the first two years of their children's lives. Participation in the program is voluntary. The weekly home visits contain a "good" parenting component, teaching childrearing and life skills. The program helps stabilize single-mother families and assists the mothers establish healthier emotional attachments to their children. The nurses strive to enhance mothers' sensitivities to their offsprings' cues, reduce the reliance on spanking as a disciplinary measure, and raise the number of age-appropriate learning materials available and the amount of time devoted to reading to the children.

The Nurse–Family Partnership program, now serving clients in some twenty-five states, with the added sites maintaining fidelity to the original model, has demonstrated a number of empirically verified, positive long-term outcomes in the criminal justice and educational achievement areas. In contrast to the fifteen-year-old adolescents born to women in the control group, those visited by nurses reported 59 percent fewer arrest and had 90 percent fewer adjudications as persons in need of supervision for incorrigible behavior.[9] The nurse-visited youth showed a trend to having fewer convictions and probation violations. The effects on crime and antisocial behavior were greater for children born to mothers at heightened risk because of their being poor and unmarried in this study. The program had, however, no impact on other antisocial behavioral problems, such as parents' or children's reports of major or minor acts of delinquency.

These regular home visits also boosted educational achievement. Nurse-visited children at age nine compared to a control group had better grade point averages and achievement test scores in math and reading in grades one through three.[10] A follow-up study of the children at age twelve in the intervention and control groups showed that the children visited by nurses scored higher on reading and math tests at that age. They also had higher achievement test scores in reading and math in grades one through six and higher grade point averages in reading and math in grades four through six.[11]

However, another study showed no impact of the program on high school graduation rates.[12]

The Nurse–Family Partnership has passed the cost-benefit test. According to one estimate, based on a follow-up analysis during the visited children's secondary school years, the program generated benefits (in 2003 dollars) of some $26,000 ($26,298) per year compared to cost of about $9,000 ($9,118) per year or $2.88 in benefits per dollar of expenditures.[13]

Backed by thirty years of empirical research studies demonstrating effectiveness and the successful multisite implementation of the Nurse–Family Partnership, the 2010 Patient Protection and Affordable Care Act includes $1.5 billion over five years in mandatory funding for the states through the Maternal, Infant, and Early Childhood Home Visitation Program to support early childhood home visiting programs. The funding is as follows: $100 million for fiscal year 2010, $250 million for fiscal year 2011, $350 million for fiscal year 2012, $400 million for fiscal year 2013, and $400 million for fiscal year 2014, with 3 percent of the amounts appropriated reserved for research and evaluation.

A Comprehensive Approach: Harlem Children's Zone

To deal with the home, school, and neighborhood environments, the Harlem Children's Zone (HCZ), Inc., founded by Geoffrey Canada in 1997, takes a comprehensive, "conveyor belt" developmental approach.[14] The HCZ provides a series of structured interventions for urban youth beginning before birth and ending hopefully with college graduation, based on the assumption that college is for everyone. Its web of holistic programs and services seek to reach almost every child growing up in a small area, some ninety-seven blocks of a struggling central Harlem neighborhood, where 73 percent of all children are born into poor families. The area has the highest rate of foster care placement in New York City and its unemployment rate is typically about double the rate of New York City, as a whole.

The HCZ has the potential to change outcomes not only for individual children and their families but also for a devastated neighborhood, one of concentrated disadvantage. Mr. Canada wants to "contaminate" the zone culture with aspirational values, a sense of hope about the future, and disciplined self-improvement, thereby creating a "tipping point" so that HCZ's programs and services positively impact on the community's environment. As he put it, "We are attempting to save a community and its kids all at the same time."[15]

HCZ provides a number of community-based services for children and their families from birth through college designed to offer a positive, supportive environment outside of formal educational settings. The community-focused approach is premised on the notion that many of the issues and challenges K-12 public schools deal with originate outside of the classroom. As discussed in Chapter 1, socioeconomic-based achievement gaps are formed and exist prior to children entering kindergarten.

The conveyor belt chain of support and linked programs moves through three main phases: Baby College, Harlem Gems, and Promise Academy 1 and 2, two charter schools, along with community after-school, health care services, and neighborhood programs. HCZ begins with Baby College, nine-week, Saturday morning, prenatal and early childhood (up to age three) parenting classes, including sessions on the importance of prenatal care, brain development, discipline and alternatives to physical punishment, parent–child bonding, and essential skills, such as reading to children.[16] To recruit mothers for Baby College, outreach workers canvas residences in the zone, knocking on every door, and stopping everyone on the street and handing out flyers.

Next, Harlem Gems, a prekindergarten program for four-year olds, modeled on other early education programs,[17] strives to develop the preliteracy and language skills needed for kindergarten. The intensive, eleven-month all-day classes, which focus on vocabulary building and include foreign language instruction, are tiny, with a four to one child-to-adult ratio. HCZ assigns a social worker to each family with a child in Harlem Gems.

At its two Promise Academy K-12 charter schools, some 1,300 students, who are admitted by lottery, arrive as early as 7:30 a.m. for a healthy breakfast and stay as late as 7:00 p.m. There is an extended school day and an eleven-month school year. Students performing below grade level spend twice as much time in school as New York City public school students. Those performing at grade level spend 50 percent more time in school. There are small class sizes, teachers' aides, and other support to facilitate teaching. In its high school, there are two licensed teachers in each classroom. It is a disciplined, orderly, demanding culture, based on academic rigor. Students are surrounded with the importance of hard work; excuses are not allowed. In addition to access to free health care services and social workers, students receive test preparation, after-school tutoring, and after-school and weekend enrichment classes. A coordinated after-school program includes a roster of academics, athletics, art, and music. HCZ follows a community school approach, offering an after-school program to students in the zone who attend regular public schools.

HCZ programs include preventive health care services, truancy prevention, and precollege advice. Its asthma initiative, for example, drastically reduced the number of emergency room visits and missed school days. HCZ-targeted initiatives, such as asthma and obesity prevention, are available to any child in the zone, even those not enrolled in one of HCZ's charter schools.[18]

HCZ's neighborhood programs include organizing block associations, refurbishing playgrounds and parks, and providing foster care prevention. It helps tenants buy apartment buildings from New York City by creating a structure to transfer city-owned buildings to resident ownership and management. It also has set up and operates community centers that bring together residents around sports, recreation, health, wellness, and the performing arts. In sum, HCZ floods the zone with an array of educational, social, and health care services to save and rebuild a community and its children at the same time.

One study showed the educational achievement benefits of HCZ's Promise Academy.[19] Researchers compared the academic outcomes of HCZ lottery winners—the intervention group—and its lottery losers—the control group—with differences in academic achievement between the two groups supposedly limited to the opportunity to enroll in an HCZ charter school. The study found a very large impact of an HCZ charter school on academic achievement, particularly in math by the end of middle school.

In an HCZ charter middle school, the eighth grade largely African-American student body, who entered the school's sixth grade two years earlier, scored nearly as high in math as the average white student in the New York City public schools, basically eliminating the achievement gap. With respect to English language arts, the HCZ students outperformed the control group and reduced the achievement gap in comparison to the average white student in the New York City public schools.[20]

This study also compared the academic achievement gains by HCZ charter school students living inside the zone's geographical boundaries and, thus, eligible for the complete package of social and community supports, with those outside the zone's boundaries who received only the charter school component. Raising doubt as to the effectiveness of the nonschool community components, these researchers found that both the inside and outside students received the same academic benefits from the HCZ charter school, with and without the social and community programs.[21]

Although other experts noted, "Thus students attending the HCZ Promise Academy are doing impressively better than students of their backgrounds attending a typical public school in NYC," research by these critics indicated that "the HCZ Promise Academy is a middling New York City charter school." They concluded, "There is no compelling evidence that investments in parenting classes, health services, nutritional programs, and community improvement in general have appreciable effects on student achievement in schools in the U.S."[22]

Because linking social services, broadly defined, to promote student achievement, as HCZ does, is expensive, this study's conclusion is important in terms of a cost-benefit analysis. The HCZ spends in class per student in its charter schools some $12,500 ($12,443) in public funds and about $3,800 ($3,842) in private funds each year. These figures do not include a variety of other expenditures, including the HCZ central administration, most building costs, the after-school program, rewards for student performance, a chef who prepares healthy meals, and facilities provided for a health clinic.[23] In total, the HCZ spends about $19,000 ($19,272) per student, per year in its charter schools. The noncharter school community programs costs about $5,000 per child per year. Given limited public and private resources, rather than attempt a transformation of an entire neighborhood, it may be better to focus on rigorous, academically oriented charter schools, such as KIPP (Knowledge Is Power Program), that have achieved notable academic successes,[24] but do not provide (or depend on) community and social services to achieve their academic mission.

Promise Neighborhoods Program

In 2010, the Promise Neighborhoods Program, modeled after the HCZ, part of the Obama administration's Neighborhood Revitalization Initiative,[25] received an initial $10 million Congressional appropriation for fiscal year 2010. Congress subsequently increased funding for the program to $30 million for fiscal year 2011.

The Obama administration, in September 2010, awarded planning grants to twenty-one groups throughout the United States in an effort to begin to transform the environment in which poor children grow up, the way families raise them and schools teach them, and the character of neighborhoods.[26] With one-year grants of up to $500,000, the recipients will create plans to provide cradle-to-career services that will not only improve the educational achievement and healthy development of children and boost family engagement in student learning but also enhance the health, safety, and stability of neighborhoods. The planning grants will support the work of a diverse set of communities in major urban areas, small- and medium-size cities, rural areas, and one Indian reservation.

At present, it is unclear whether multisite programs modeled after HCZ that seek to make up for familial and neighborhood deficits and to change an entire area, can work without the leadership of HCZ's charismatic founder, Geoffrey Canada. The nationwide replication and success of these various programs depends, in part, on each community's capacity to take the HCZ elements and then adapt and reconfigure them along other strategies from research and experience, as appropriate in the new setting.

Estimates indicate that full implementation by the twenty-one grantees of their own zones will cost the federal government an additional $200 million, thus a request by the Obama administration of $210 million in fiscal year 2011, $200 million to support the implementation of Promise Neighborhoods projects and $10 million for planning grants for new communities. Implementation by the twenty-one grantees will likely require an additional $200 million in private funds, necessitating an innovative public–private partnership.

Rethinking the War on Drugs

In coming decades, policymakers must also rethink the War on Drugs. At some point, I believe, the American public will conclude that the drug war has failed as did prohibition. The War on Drugs has not ended (or even significantly reduced) drug usage.[27]

The negative consequences of the War on Drugs abound. As discussed in Chapter 1, the drug war has imprisoned many, particularly black males, who in my opinion, should not be behind bars. Interdiction has made drugs more expensive, raising profit margins and fueling a multibillion dollar, criminal industry in drug delivery and sales. It has increased the incidence of crime with many property offenses—robberies and burglaries—resulting from the inflated drug costs caused by criminalization. It also has helped to create gangs.

In reconsidering the War on Drugs, policymakers must balance the costs (and other negative consequences) of drug prohibition against the risk of legalization (or at least the decriminalization of nonviolent drug offenses) of not only possession, but also distribution. In addition to reducing crime and the violence associated with drug markets, legalization would decrease public sector expenditures on enforcement and raise revenue.[28] One report estimates that legalizing drugs would save about $41.3 billion per year in public expenditures on enforcing drug prohibition in the United States, including police, judicial, legal, and correction expenses. About $8.7 billion of the savings would accrue from the legalization of marijuana and $32.6 from the legalization of other drugs (heroin, cocaine, and synthetics). Of these savings, $25.7 billion would flow to state and local governments; $15.6 billion would accrue to the federal government.

Drug legalization would, in addition, yield tax revenues estimated at $46.7 billion per year, assuming the legal drugs were taxed at rates comparable to those placed on alcohol and tobacco. About $8.7 billion would result from the legalization of marijuana; $38.0 billion from the legalization of other drugs.

The public sector could redirect the expenditure savings and the added revenues, in part, to effective drug education to discourage drug use and to the treatment of drug addicts in a cost-effective manner.[29] In formulating approaches to drug education designed to reduce drug usage, policymakers could look to existing public health strategies to reduce tobacco and alcohol consumption. Funds could also go to comprehensive approaches to human capital development, such as the Promise Neighborhoods Program, provided a national, multisite evaluation clearly demonstrates its effectiveness.

On the downside, it is unclear whether legalization (or decriminalization) would make experimentation and dabbling more common, especially among young people, possibly leading to the ravages of higher addiction rates. Because drug users often begin with marijuana and then go to more powerful drugs, a legalization (or decriminalization) strategy ought to start with marijuana and assess its impact in terms of usage, and then progress to cocaine, heroin, and synthetics.

Taking the profits out of drugs, beginning with marijuana, would likely shrink gangs, their size, power and violence, and reduce crime levels. Fewer addicts would commit property crimes to pay for their habit; treatment slots would increase. Ultimately, complete (or nearly complete) legalization (or decriminalization) would likely devastate major drug trafficking organizations. Mexico, among other countries, would thank us. However, it is unclear whether these organizations would go into other activities, such as kidnapping, oil theft, pirated goods, extortion, and continue to flourish.[30]

Even with complete (or nearly complete) legalization (or decriminalization), drug sales to minors ought to remain illegal. Driving under the influence of drugs would be illegal. Employers could make drug testing a condition of employment, retention, and discharge with drug policy a matter of collective bargaining agreements in unionized workplaces and collaborative development between employers and employees in nonunionized organizations.

In the meantime, policymakers ought to focus on drug treatment, not long-term incarceration, for nonviolent low-level offenders.[31] As part of broader, spending-reduction efforts, this approach is less expensive and likely to be far more effective than aggressively prosecuting drug offenders who then cycle in and out of correctional facilities.

Notes

1. Nathan Glazer, "Notes on the State of Black America," *American Interest* 5, no. 6 (July/August 2010): 110–16, at 116.
2. Richard H. Thaler and Cass R. Sunstein, *Nudge: Improving Decisions about Health, Wealth, and Happiness* (New Haven, CT: Yale University Press, 2008).
3. Public Law 104-193. For an overview of the welfare reform provisions with respect to marriage and two-parent families see Gene Falk and Jill Tauber, "Welfare Reform: TANF Provisions Related to Marriage and Two-Parent Families," CRS Report for Congress, October 30, 2001, RL 31170; Britt Ehrhardt and Karen Spar, "Welfare Reform: TANF Activities to Reduce Nonmarital Pregnancy," CRS Report to Congress, December 18, 2001, RL 31219, provided an overview of welfare reform provisions to reduce nonmarital childbearing. See also U.S. General Accounting Office, "Welfare Reform: More Research Needed on TANF Family Caps and Other Policies for Reducing Out-of-Wedlock Births," September 2001, GAO-01-924.
4. Public Law 109-171.
5. Kathryn Edin and Maria Kefalas, *Promises I Can Keep: Why Poor Women Put Motherhood Before Marriage* (Berkeley, CA: University of California Press, 2005), 109–37. See also Kathryn Edin, "What Do Low-Income Single Mothers Say about Marriage," *Social Problems* 47, no. 1 (February 2000): 112–33, at 117–30; Kathryn Edin, "Few Good Men: Why Poor Mothers Don't Marry or Remarry," *American Prospect* 11, no. 4 (January 3, 2000): 26–31.
6. Barack Obama, "Remarks at a Townhall Meeting on Fatherhood and a Questions-and-Answer Session," June 19, 2009; Barack Obama, *Public Papers of the Presidents of the United States 2009*, Book 1—January 20 to June 30, 2009 (Washington, DC: Government Printing Office, 2010), 857–63; Barack Obama, "We Need Fathers to Step Up," *Parade*, June 21, 2009, 4–5.

See also Helene Cooper, "President Delivers Exhortation to Fathers," *New York Times*, June 20, 2009, A10.

7.   Maureen R. Waller, "Viewing Low-Income Fathers' Ties to Families through a Cultural Lens: Insights for Research and Policy," *Annals of the American Academy of Political and Social Science* 629 (May 2010): 102–24, at 108–12. See also Maureen R. Waller, *My Baby's Father: Unmarried Parents and Paternal Responsibility* (Ithaca, NY: Cornell, 2002), 48–69.

8.   For background on the Nurse–Family Partnership see David L. Olds, "The Nurse-Family Partnership," in *The Crisis in Youth Mental Health: Critical Issues and Effective Programs*, Vol. 4, *Early Intervention Programs and Policies*, ed. Norman Watt et al. (Westport, CT: Praeger, 2006), 147–80; David L. Olds and others, "Programs for Parents of Infants and Toddlers: Recent Evidences from Randomized Trials," *Journal of Child Psychology and Psychiatry* 48, no. 3–4 (March/April 2007): 355–91, at 376–81; David Olds, "The Nurse-Family Partnership," in *Investing in Young Children: New Directions in Federal Preschool and Early Childhood Policy*, ed. Ron Haskins and W. Steven Barnett (Washington, DC: Brookings Institution and National Institute for Early Education Research, 2010), 69–77. For a journalist account of the Nurse–Family Partnership see Katherine Boo, "Swamp Nurse," *New Yorker* 81, no. 46 (February 6, 2006): 54–65; Olds and others, "Programs for Parents of Infants and Toddlers," 362–76, summarized the empirical evidence of other home visiting programs designed to promote child health and development.

9.   David Olds and others, "Long-Term Effects of Nurse Home Visitation on Children's Criminal and Antisocial Behavior: 15-year Follow-Up of a Randomized Controlled Trial," *Journal of the American Medical Association* 280, no. 14 (October 14, 1998): 1238–44, at 1241–43. A subsequent article, John Echenrode and others, "Long-Term Effects of Prenatal and Infancy Nurse Home Visitation on the Life Course of Youths," *Archives of Pediatrics & Adolescent Medicine* 164, no. 1 (January 2010): 9–16, at 12–13, showed fewer lifetime arrests and convictions for females but not for males in the intervention group compared with those in the control group. See also Peter W. Greenwood, *Changing Lives: Delinquency Prevention as Crime-Control Policy* (Chicago, IL: University of Chicago Press, 2006), 13, 37, 52, 79, 142.

10. David L. Olds and others, "Effects of Nurse Home Visiting on Maternal and Child Functioning: Age-9 Follow-Up of a Randomized Trial," *Pediatrics* 120, no. 4 (October 2007): e832–e845, at e841–e842. Another study, John Holmberg and others, "Teacher Data for the Denver Year-9 Follow-Up," in David Olds and others, "Impact of the Nurse-Family Partnership on Neighborhood Context," Government Expenditures, and Children's School Functioning, U.S. Department of Justice, Document No. 233277, January 2011, found no statistically significant program effects on grade point averages in reading and math.

11. Harriet J. Kitzman and others, "Enduring Effects of Prenatal and Infancy Home Visiting by Nurses on Children: Follow-Up of a Randomized Trial among Children at Age 12 Years," *Archives of Pediatrics & Adolescent Medicine* 164, no. 5 (May 2010): 412–18, at 41–418.

12. Eckenrode and others, "Long-Term Effects," 13.

13. Steve Aos and others, "Benefits and Costs of Prevention and Early Intervention Programs for Youth," Washington State Institute for Public Policy, September 17, 2004, Document No. 04-07-3901, 6 (Table 1 Summary of Benefits and Costs [2003 Dollars]).

14. Harlem Children's Zone (HCZ), "History," http://www.hcz.org/about-us/history (accessed November 12, 2010); "Our Results," http://www.hcz.org/our-results (accessed November 12, 2010); HCZ, "An Investment in Success: 2008–2009 Biennial Report"; "Harlem Children's Zone: A Look Inside" (College Success Office, Spring 2008, The Countee Cullen Beacon [New Vision after School Program] Summer 2006, TRUCE [The Renaissance University for Community Education] Spring 2006, The Peacemakers, Fall 2004, Community Pride, Spring 2003, The Baby College, Summer/Fall 2002); HCZ, "Growth Plan FY 2001–FY2009," updated Fall 2003. See generally, Paul Tough, *Whatever It Takes: Geoffrey Canada's Quest to Change Harlem and America* (Boston, MA: Houghton Mifflin, 2008). See also Robin Shulman, "Harlem Program Singled Out as Model," *Washington Post*, August 2, 2009, A3; David Brooks, "The Harlem Miracle," *New York Times*, May 8, 2009, A21; Nichole Perlroth, "Cloning Geoff Canada," *Forbes* 185, no. 4 (March 29, 2010): 54.

15. Sharon Otterman, "Despite Money and Attention, It's Not All A's at 2 Harlem Schools," *New York Times*, October 13, 1010, A18.

16. For a summary of empirical research on other promising perinatal interventions see Olds and others, "Programs for Parents," 360–62.

17. A detailed analysis of early childhood interventions, such as Head Start, is beyond the scope of this book. In brief, these early childhood interventions boost kindergarten readiness, but the academic achievement benefits vanish as black children enter elementary school. See, e.g., Michael Puma and others, "Head Start Impact Study: Final Report, U.S. Department of Health and Human Services, Administration for Children and Families," Office of Planning, Research and Evaluation, January 2010, xvi, xxiii, xxv, 4-15, 4-18, 4-25 to 4-27, 4-30 to 4-32; David Deming, "Early Childhood Intervention and Life-Cycle Skill Development: Evidence from Head Start," *American Economic Journal* 1, no. 3 (July 2009): 111–34, at 112, 116–17, 123–24, 126; Janet Currie and Duncan Thomas, "Does Head Start Make a Difference?" *American Economic Review* 85, no. 3 (June 1995): 341–64. See also Haskins and Barnett, "New Directions for America's Early Childhood Policies," in *Investing in Young Children*, 8–9; Joe Klein, "Head Start Doesn't Work," *Time* 18, no. 3 (July 18, 2011): 27. Early childhood programs may achieve positive long-term outcomes for blacks, including improving high school graduation rates, reducing crime, and enhancing labor market outcomes. Deming, "Early Childhood Intervention," 112, 126; Eliana Garces and others, "Longer Term Effects of Head Start," *American Economic Review* 92, no. 4 (September 2002): 999–1012, at 1009. Head Start likely raises noncognitive skills, such as motivation, self-discipline, persistence, and dependability, thereby promoting later success in social and economic life. James J. Heckman and others, "The Effects of Cognitive and Noncognitive Abilities on Labor Market Outcomes and Social Behavior," *Journal of Labor Economics* 24, no. 3 (July 2006): 411–82, at 478. For a favorable overview of early childhood programs see Lynn A. Karoly and others, "Early

Childhood Interventions: Proven Results, Future Promise," RAND Labor and Population, 2005.

18. For a complete list of HCZ community programs see Will Dobbie and Ronald G. Fryer, Jr., "Are High-Quality Schools Enough to Increase Achievement among the Poor? Evidence from the Harlem Children's Zone," May 2010, Appendix A: Complete List of Harlem Children's Zone Programs.

19. Dobbie and Fryer, "Are High-Quality Schools Enough to Increase Achievement Amount the Poor? Evidence from the Harlem Children's Zone," *American Economic Journal: Applied Economics* 3, no. 3 (July 2010): 158–87.

20. Ibid., 160, 171, 179.

21. Ibid., 160–61, 176, 179–80.

22. The quotations in this paragraph are from Grover J. Whitehurst and Michelle Croft, "The Harlem Children's Zone, Promise Neighborhoods, and the Broader, Bolder Approach to Education," Brown Center on Education Policy, Brookings Institution, July 20, 2010, 6, 7, 8. For a critique of the Whitehurst–Croft report see Geoffrey Canada, "The Harlem Children's Zone Response to the Brookings Institute's Report: 'The Harlem Children's Zone, Promise Neighborhoods, and the Broader, Bolder Approach to Education,'" n.d.

23. The statistics in this paragraph are from Otterman, "Despite Money" and Shulman, "Harlem Program."

24. The KIPP network of some ninety-nine charter schools in twenty states and the District of Columbia rely on providing a safe, structured environment, strict behavior norms, a strong student work ethic, more time in school (including a longer school day and school year), and selecting teachers in the basis of ability, not seniority. KIPP, "What is a KIPP School?" http://www. kipp.org/01/whatisakippschool.cfm (accessed December 1, 2008). See also Paul Tough, "What It Takes to Make a Student," *New York Times Magazine*, November 26, 2006, 44–51, 69–71, 73; Joshua D. Angrist and others, "Who Benefits from KIPP?" National Bureau of Economic Research, February 2010, NBER Working Paper 15740; Joshua D. Angrist and others, "Inputs and Impacts in Charter Schools: KIPP Lynn," *American Economic Review* 100, no. 2 (May 2010): 239–43; Christina Clark Tuttle and others, "Student Characteristics and Achievement in 22 KIPP Middle Schools," Mathematica Policy Research, Final Report, June 2010; Katrina R. Woodworth and others, "San Francisco Bay Area KIPP Schools: A Study of Early Implementation and Achievement," Center for Education Policy, SRI International, Final Report, 2008.

25. The White House Neighborhood Revitalization Initiative, n.d., http://www. whitehouse.gov/sites/default/files/nri.description.pdf, which seeks to align federal housing, education, justice, and health programs to transform neighborhoods of concentrated disadvantage.

26. U.S. Department of Education, Press Release, "U.S. Department of Education Awards Promise Neighborhoods Planning Grants," September 21, 2010. For background on the Promise Neighborhoods Program see Harlem Children's Zone, Center for the Study of Social Policy, PolicyLink, Focusing on Results in *Promise Neighborhoods:* Recommendations for the Federal Initiative, January 2010, that provided a suggested results framework and Child Trends, Results and Indicators for Children: An Analysis

to Inform Discussion About Promise Neighborhoods, November 6, 2009, synthesizing research about the factors contributing to children's healthy development, academic success, and college graduation. See also Lisbeth Schorr, "Realizing President Obama's Promise to Scale Up What Works to Fight Urban Poverty," Center for the Study of Social Policy, revised, June 2009. In its budget for fiscal year 2012, the Obama administration sought $150 million for the Promise Neighborhoods Program, down from $210 million it requested for fiscal year 2011. Office of Management and Budget, Fiscal Year 2012 Budget of the U.S. Government, 70 and Office of Management and Budget, Budget of the U.S. Government Year 2011, 26.

27. For a critique on the War on Drugs see Report of the Global Commission on Drug Policy, War On Drugs, June 2011; George P. Shultz and Paul A. Volcker, "A Real Debate about Drug Policy," *Wall Street Journal*, June 11, 2011, C2; Jimmy Carter, "Call Off the Global Drug War," *New York Times*, June 17, 2011, A31; Mary Anastasia O'Grady, "More Calls for a Drug War Cease-Fire," *Wall Street Journal*, June 6, 2011, A17. But see Joseph A. Califano, Jr. and William A. Bennett, "Do We Really Want a 'Needle Park' on American Soil?" *Wall Street Journal*, July 1, 2011, A15.

28. Jeffrey A. Miron and Katherine Waldock, "The Budgetary Impact of Ending Drug Prohibition," Cato Institute, 2010, 1–12. The revenue estimate are subject to various unknowns, such as the market price of marijuana and exactly how to tax marijuana. See also Rosalie Liccardo Pacula, "Examining the Impact of Marijuana Legalization on Harms Associated with Marijuana Use," RAND Drug Policy Research Center, July 2010, WR-769-RC, 25–26, concluding that the health care expenditures associated with legalization of marijuana in California would likely be small relative to the expected revenue gains and cost savings, but recognizing the potential for significant health care expenditures resulting from the impact of marijuana on mental health and drugged driving.

29. Drug prevention programs can be cost effective, but may not, however, be very effective. Mark A. R. Kleinman and others, *Drugs and Drug Policy: What Everyone Needs to Know* (New York: Oxford University Press, 2011), 75–77.

30. Sylvia Longmire, "Legalization Won't Kill Cartels," *New York Times*, June 19, 2011, Week in Review Section, 10; Anthony Harrup and David Luhnow, "Mexican Crime Groups Use Stolen Oil to Fuel Enterprise," *Wall Street Journal*, June 18–19, 2011, A11.

31. See, e.g., Pew Center on the States, *One in 31: The Long Reach of American Corrections* (Washington, DC: Pew Charitable Trusts, March 2009), 22–30. See also Charlie Savage, "Trend to Lighten Harsh Sentences Catches on in Conservative States," *New York Times*, August 13, 2011, A14. Nathan Koppel and Gary Fields, "States Rethink Drugs Laws," *Wall Street Journal*, March 5–6, 2011, A3; Gary Fields, "States Seek Prison Breaks," *Wall Street Journal*, February 8, 2011, A3; David A. Boyum and Mark A. R. Kleinman, "Substance Abuse Policy from a Crime-Control Perspective," in *Crime: Public Policies For Crime Control*, ed. James Q. Wilson and Joan Petersilia (Oakland, CA: ICS Press, 2002), 331–82.

Index